A MIDDLE ENGLISH TREATISE ON THE PLAYING OF MIRACLES

Edited by
Clifford Davidson
Western Michigan University

University Press of America

Copyright © 1981 by
University Press of America, Inc.™
P.O. Box 19101, Washington, DC 20036

All rights reserved
Printed in the United States of America

ISBN: 0-8191-1515-0 Perfect
0-8191-1514-2 Case
Library of Congress Number: 81-40028

ACKNOWLEDGEMENTS

This edition of the Wycliffite treatise on the playing of miracles is intended to fill the need for a practical and readily available presentation of Middle English dramatic criticism for those who are interested in medieval drama and theater. As such, it is an outgrowth of the Early Drama, Art, and Music project sponsored by The Medieval Institute, and is designed as a supplement to EDAM publications being issued by Medieval Institute Publications. I am therefore most grateful to the University Press of America for its willingness to make this material available.

In the process of preparing this modest volume, I owe a great deal to many colleagues on both sides of the Atlantic. Curiously, however, my greatest debt may perhaps be to the librarians at the University of Michigan Graduate Library, for it was there that I first encountered almost a decade ago the article by Lawrence G. Craddock who most forcefully made me aware of the importance of the *Tretise of Miraclis Pleyinge* as well as of other critical writings on drama from the medieval period. Craddock's article sent me eventually back to V. A. Kolve's book, which I had not sufficiently appreciated when it was first published. In my work toward understanding the aesthetic of medieval drama, my own thinking has often been paralleled and extended by Theresa Coletti, whose dissertation on the devotional image and medieval drama was early brought to my attention and whose work-in-progress in this area is scheduled for publication in the EDAM monograph series. I am also most grateful to Nicholas Davis of the University of Liverpool, whose dissertation came to my notice late in this project and whose comments have been invaluable. Robert Palmatier, Chairman of the Linguistics Department at Western Michigan University, provided advice toward the principles utilized in lightly regularizing the spelling in order to provide a more widely usable edition (the letters þ and ȝ as well as j, i, y, u, and v have been regularized throughout according to modern usage), and also gave helpful suggestions toward the preparation of the glossary. Naturally, I am also aware of indebtedness to previous editors of the *Tretise*, especially of course to Anne Hudson, whose recent *English Wycliffite*

Writings contains a portion of the text; all who have gone before have made my work easier.

I am also grateful to the librarians at the British Library, Western Michigan University Libraries, the Bodleian Library, the Cambridge University Library, and the University of Chicago Library. Support for research on the *Tretise* was generously given through a summer research fellowship and a grant from Western Michigan University, and my department kindly provided released time from teaching during one semester so that the task could be completed. Also, I have received generous aid through the EDAM project and the Medieval Institute for the preparation of camera-ready copy, especially through the assistance of Debra Rycenga, editorial assistant.

The text of the *Tretise of Miraclis Pleyinge* and also the text of the poem "On the Minorite Friars" included in the Introduction are presented here through the courtesy of the British Library.

CONTENTS

Acknowledgements iii

Introduction 1

A Tretise of Miraclis Pleyinge 35

Textual Notes 57

Critical Notes 59

Glossary 79

vi

INTRODUCTION

It is curious that the most important piece of dramatic criticism in Middle English should be a hostile Wycliffite tract which attempts to turn all the power of its polemic against the playing of *miracles*, a term that appears to cover the whole range of religious drama though the playing of the Passion is regarded as particularly reprehensible. The treatise contained in British Library MS. Add. 24,202, fols. 14-21, presents in the midst of its attack on the stage also what must be regarded as a fairly coherent argument in their defense. Hence Rosemary Woolf was led to suggest that this Wycliffite treatise may have been "replying to some corresponding Latin treatise in defense of mystery plays" much in the manner of the attack, contained in another treatise in the same manuscript (fols. 26-28^v), upon Walter Hilton's Latin treatise defending images.[1] Whether or not such a Latin defense of the plays ever existed, the evidence of *A Treatise of Miraclis Pleyinge* nevertheless establishes a well thought out aesthetic basis for the religious stage of the late Middle Ages. Thus, as V. A. Kolve notes, the long accepted view that these religious plays were naive and lacking in "theory" can hardly be sustained.[2] The importance of the Wycliffite treatise for students of the early drama can hardly be over-estimated, for it contains a view of drama that quite simply makes sense of much other available evidence concerning the religious stage and the presentation of the late medieval vernacular drama. Additionally, the treatise's arguments against the religious stage also have a real interest for us since these help us to chart the pattern of religious hostility to the theater which culminated in the closing of the playhouses in England in 1642.

The *Tretise of Miraclis Pleyinge* is in two parts, possibly not even written by the same author, but it is the first part that summarizes six points in favor of the dramatic presentation of scenes of a religious nature:

> 1. Plays are presented for the service and worship of God.

2. Through these scenes, men see the consequences of sin and are converted.

3. Men and women are brought to pious tears by the sight of Christ's Passion in dramatic representation; such a reaction is not in the spirit of mockery.

4. Some men can only be converted by means of entertainment--i.e., "by gamen and pley."

5. Recreation is necessary for all men, and this kind of recreation is better than any other.

6. It is permitted to paint the wondrous deeds of Christ and his saints; therefore, why should these not be presented in plays which are more vivid than mere painting?[3]

Needless to say, the entire purpose of the first part of the Wycliffite treatise is to refute these arguments in favor of playing religious drama, while the second part of the treatise turns its attention to a Wycliffite sympathizer who nevertheless sees value from an educational standpoint in plays on sacred subjects.

The Wycliffite treatise is thus broadly opposed to the practice of the medieval stage as it attempted to set forth events from sacred history within the context of religious festivals. From the beginning to the end of the treatise the true miracles of Christ and his apostles are contrasted with the pretense of the theatrical "miraclis"; the first were done "in ernest," the second merely "in pley and bourde." Significantly the writer's attitude toward play, particularly when religious matters are involved, remains throughout harsh and lacking in sympathy. The view of life which is implied is rigidly ascetic and puritan, and indeed looks forward to the total rejection of the stage by the more zealous protestants of the sixteenth and seventeenth centuries. It also is of a piece with the protestant and humanist attack on religious drama in the Reformation period--an attack described by Father Gardiner in his well known study, *Mysteries' End*.[4]

Hostility to drama, as everyone knows, had been a characteristic of the Christian Church during the Patristic era, for which Tertullian perhaps spoke most authoritatively in his *De Spectaculis*. For Tertullian the stage was devil-inspired,[5] an idea that returns in the Wycliffite treatise. To *see* stage plays is self-indulgence in wicked sights which cannot be viewed without harm to the soul. Christians, says Tertullian,

> are bidden to put away from us all impurity. By this command we are cut off once for all from the theatre, the proper home of all impurity, where nothing wins approval but what elsewhere has no approval.[6]

In the final analysis Tertullian must describe the stage as "so much honey dropping from a poisoned bit of pastry."[7] For the Wycliffite writer, however, the most horrifying spectacle was to see sacred events mimicked on stage allegedly for religious edification; the presentation of secular scenes, albeit at times less than edifying, would be far less reprehensible, he claims. Hence the playing of miracles is said to be "worse than thou[gh] they pleyiden pure vaniteis"; he insists that it is normally less wicked "to pleyin rebaudye than to pleyin siche miriclis."

The early Christian attitude toward theatrical spectacle as associated with sexual immorality is not far beneath the surface of the Wycliffite treatise, which charges that "miraclis pleyinge is of the lustis of the fleyssh and mirthe of the body." Isidore of Seville had associated the theater with prostitution--an association that was still to be reckoned with in Shakespeare's time.[8] Isidore's comments are, as Mary Marshall has shown, repeated through the Middle Ages; Chaucer's statement in translating Boethius--"These comune strompettis of swich a place that men clepen the theatre"-- may be taken as typical.[9] Ovidian treatises on the art of love from the Middle Ages include plays among those places where young lovers are most likely to make "progress" with ladies.[10] Later, in 1493, the woodcut showing the theater in the *Terence* printed by Trechsel at Lyons also shows activities in the lower part of the illustration that are appropriate to a brothel.[11]

Medieval antagonism toward drama, even to liturgical drama and quasi-dramatic ritual forms, has often been noted.

Gerhoh of Reichersberg in the twelfth century denounced the practices of the monks of Augsburg, who he said needed the inducement of a representation of such a scene as the Slaughter of the Innocents if they were to sup in the refectory. These plays and spectacles were roundly condemned by Gerhoh, who also suggested in his later *De Investigatione Antichristi* (c.1161) that clerics who transform the church into a theater are themselves doing the works of the same Antichrist whose works are the subject of the spectacle being presented.[12] Plays are said to be false and empty vanities, for they give precise form to sacred events in ways that deserve only condemnation. It is the *illusion* that is being rejected here—the same principle that was similarly controversial in the visual arts during this period. The tendency toward verisimilitude or realism was particularly distrusted, both in drama and the pictorial arts. Additionally, the element of *game* was found particularly noxious, for Gerhoh, like the later Wycliffite writer responsible for *A Tretise of Miraclis Pleyinge*, saw stage spectacle as presenting an illicit form of *pleasurable* experience.

Thus Herrad of Landsberg also laments the abuses of the presentation of the *Stella* in the twelfth century:

> But what nowadays happens in many churches? Not a customary ritual, not an act of reverence, but one of irreligion and extravagance conducted with all the license of youth. The priests having changed their clothes go forth as a troop of warriors; there is no distinction between priest and warrior to be marked. At an unfitting gathering of priests and laymen the church is desecrated by feasting and drinking, buffoonery, unbecoming jokes, play, the clang of weapons, the presence of shameless wenches, the vanities of the world, and all sorts of disorder.[13]

All of this is said to stand in contrast to the decorum of the ritual forms established for Epiphany by the Church Fathers, whose care was for the strengthening of belief and the attracting of unbelievers rather than for entertainment.[14] As in the view of the Wycliffite writer, the harmful elements in drama include mimicry, comedy, play, and lack of seriousness.

In twelfth-century England, Aelred of Rievaulx complained of the theatricality of the liturgy of his time, since in his eyes it had become more of a spectacle than a service of prayer. The gestures and emotional effects which had been adopted were, he felt, more appropriate to the theater than to worship.[15] Aelred, as a Cistercian abbot during the early history of the order, naturally shared the ideals of the Cistercian movement, which likewise aimed at simplicity in the adornment of their churches and at a rejection of ostentatious decoration. In the windows of their churches they therefore adopted plain grisaille glass, which avoided the kind of pictorial display so familiar elsewhere. Examples of this kind of glass remain, most splendidly in the Five Sisters Window in York Minster. For a reform movement such as the Cistercians, therefore, a strong rejection of actual visual representations either in the visual arts or by living performers would seem to have been the rule. Yet it is significant that even Aelred, following St. Bernard, admitted the important role of *mental* images in devotion; addressing a novice, he wrote:

> I feel my son, I feel the same, how familiarly, how affectionately, with what tears, you seek after Jesus Himself in your holy prayers, when this sweet image of this sweet Boy appears before the eyes of your heart, when you paint this most lovely face with, as it were, a spiritual imagination, when you feel His most lovely and at the same time mild eyes radiate sweetly at you.[16]

To *play* such a scene with living actors, however, would not be allowed.

Prohibitions against secular entertainments were, of course, hardly novel before the twelfth and thirteenth centuries. The Council of Nicaea in 787 had specifically proclaimed that the life of an actor was unrighteous,[17] and in 789, for example, an episcopal edict indicated corporal punishment as appropriate for any actors (*histriones*) who put on the clothing of priests, nuns, or monks.[18] The Anglo-Saxon King Edgar in 969 accusingly noted that "a house of clergy is known . . . as a meeting place for actors . . . where mimes sing and dance."[19] Such performances had been (and continued to be) forbidden,[20] though of course we know that in England they are recorded up to the dissolution of

5

the monasteries. What is interesting is that in the twelfth and thirteenth centuries sacred drama seems very much capable of being also included in the general prohibitions against playing. Such was the case with the orders issued by Robert Grosseteste, Bishop of Lincoln, in 1236-44; here secular entertainments are lumped together with the celebration of the Feast of Fools and plays, including miracle plays.[21]

In spite of the Church Fathers' insistence on the contrast between the false spectacles of the stage and the true spectacle of the Mass, however, Honorius of Autun about the year 1000 nevertheless felt justified in comparing the sacred rites of the Church to the playing of tragedies. The celebrant is a "tragedian" who "represents" Christ's Passion as well as his victory over death to those who look on. When he extends "his hands he delineates the stretching out of Christ on the cross," for example. Thus also the Preface signifies "the cry of Christ hanging on the cross," while the secret prayers of the Canon represent in some sense the "silence of the Sabbath" or Holy Saturday. Finally, according to Honorius, the giving of "peace and communion" to the congregation by the priest is possible "because, when our accuser has been overthrown by our champion in the conflict, peace is announced by the judge to the people [who] are invited to a feast."[22] Honorius was a disciple of Amalarius of Metz, whose importance for modern dramatic criticism has been argued by O. B. Hardison, Jr.[23]

That mimesis in religious plays[24] was coming more and more by the twelfth century to be accepted is, however, indicated not only by extant dramatic texts such as the Anglo-Norman *Adam* and *La Seinte Resureccion*, but also by other evidence of the kind presented by William Fitzstephen's comment on the religious plays of London. In Fitzstephen's *Life of Thomas of Canterbury*, he praises the city of London for its sacred spectacles which were set forth on feast days in order to show miracles and martyrdoms.[25] While there is no way of ascertaining how such dramatic forms during this period departed from ritual, evidence concerning their transitional nature nevertheless is convincing. That there was then a resurgence of interest in theater is also indicated by the evidence presented through Ernst Curtius' study of theatrical metaphors, which were revived during the twelfth century.[26]

The understanding of drama as properly *devotional* in character is established by the Anglo-Norman writer William of Waddington in his *Manuel des Péchés* of the late thirteenth century. Yet William rejects open-air plays as distinguished from liturgical drama, and especially denounces the use of masks. Though those who organize such outdoor plays claim they are for the edification of the people, they are in fact, according to William, the work of the devil. Nevertheless, dramatic forms that are not actually detached from ritual are allowed and serve a devotional purpose.[27] In his English adaptation of the *Manuel des Péchés*, Robert Mannyng of Brunne, while reducing the idea of *devotion* to the more narrow *inspiring of belief* as a major purpose of the drama, otherwise accepts on the whole William's argument. His adaptation of William's text is as follows:

> hit is forbode him, in the decre,
> Miracles for to make or se;
> For, miracles yif thou byginne,
> Hit is a gadering, a sight of sinne.
>
> He may in the cherche, thurgh this resun,
> Pley the resurrecciun,--
> That is to seye, how God ros,
> God and man in might and los,--
> To make men be in beleve gode
> That he rose with flesshe and blode;
> And he may pleye withoutyn plight
> howe God was bore in yole night,
> To make men to beleve stedfastly
> That he light in the virgine Mary.
>
> Yif thou do hit in weyys or grevys,
> A sight of sinne truly hit semys.
> Seint Ysodre, I take to wittnes,
> For he hit seith, that sothe hit es;
> thus hit seith, in his boke,
> They forsake that they toke--
> God and here cristendam--
> That make swyche pleyys to any man
> As miracles and bourdys,
> Or tournamentys of grete pris.[28]

Harsh on what he believes to be unauthorized theatricals, he nevertheless approves the *playing* of the Resurrection (probably liturgical plays on the Visit of the Three Marys to the Sepulchre) and Incarnation within the Church. For his condemnation of churchyard playing and games (often presented or participated in on the north or devil's side of the church building), he calls upon the authority of Isidore of Seville. His attempt at making distinctions is indicative of the fact that through the later Middle Ages the liturgical plays continued to be acted in monastic settings, while in another kind of setting a quite different kind of religious drama had also emerged. The latter--vernacular plays on religious topics--are, of course, no longer today seen as the result of an evolutionary process by which they are supposed to have grown out of the liturgical drama; rather, their source appears to be quite separate, perhaps to a large degree deriving from the *tableaux vivants* associated with religious processions.[29] For this reason they would appear to be more closely related to the visual arts than to ritual, as the Wycliffite treatise seems to recognize when the writer notes the orthodox argument that defends the plays as a more lively kind of visual representation than painting. Indeed, the theory that at least the civic cycles in England might have had their origin in *tableaux vivants* would appear to make very good sense, since only thus can we explain the rise of wagon stages and processional production, though of course we need to be aware that fixed stages were also used.[30] In any case, we do need to look at these vernacular plays through the concept of *devotion* which, derived from popular urban piety, provided their principal animating force. Yet it is a concept that, as Robert Mannyng's text suggests, tended to become obscured among English speaking people. Thus the author of the Wycliffite *Tretise of Miraclis Pleyinge* likewise thought that the stated purpose of the plays was to bring people around to belief and to sustain them in that belief. In Wycliffite terms, the plays were to "convert" people to the faith.

It is clear that by the time that the Wycliffite treatise was written, much but not all of the early Christian hostility toward vernacular drama had dissipated. Vernacular plays by then clearly had the support of civic leaders and the clergy alike, and productions very likely involved close collaboration between citizens and clerics, particularly those associated with urban churches. As early as 1220 a production "by masked actors, as usual" at Beverley north

of the church during the summer presented the story of the
Resurrection; the crowd which gathered around, forming in
"a ring (corona)," was said to be motivated "by delight or
curiosity or devotion."[31] In 1426, the Franciscan preacher
William Melton is reported to have come to York where "in
several sermons [he] recommended the Corpus Christi play to
the people, affirming that it was good in itself and highly
praiseworthy," though admittedly the festival atmosphere
which accompanied the staging of sacred scenes also encouraged some unruliness among strangers to the city. Presumably there were those who came to the city "not for the
play alone";[32] nevertheless, that fact need not cause us to
doubt the motives of those who truly came to see the drama.
These individuals came surely for the same reasons ascribed
to the spectators at the Beverley play two hundred years be-
fore--i.e., for delight, curiosity, devotion. Because the
Register of the York cycle is extant,[33] we are able to as-
certain that its major purpose was indeed devotional, though
its inherent dramatic interest also would inspire delight
and its dramatic form would draw forth curiosity. Per-
formed on a major feast day, Corpus Christi, by guilds under the surveillance of a city corporation motivated by
piety,[34] these plays at York as elsewhere aimed at a serious religious function under the façade of play and game.
At Chester, the cycle plays were reported to have carried
the benefit of indulgences for those "that resorted peace-
ably to see the . . . plays."[35]

      In spite of the Wycliffite writer's sneer about the
weeping of spectators watching a play presumably of the Passion, such empathy with the hero of the Christian drama was
a mark of Northern peity in the late Middle Ages.[36] Margery
Kempe's uncontrollable weeping in response to the sight of
an Our Lady of Pity was different in degree only and not in
kind from what was considered acceptable behavior during
this period.[37] Emotionalism was widely encouraged, and sig-
nified a healthy inward reaction to the sight of images
which themselves carried the reality of the divine story into one's consciousness through the senses. The model for
the individual's reaction to the Passion was, after all,
the Virgin Mother herself--a powerful argument which the
Wycliffite writer is at pains to counter. The Blessed Virgin was a figure who appeared prominently in a pose of sor-
row in Flemish painting when her response to the suffering
of her Son was being characterized. Such is the case in the

triptych by Roger van der Weyden in the Gemäldegalerie, Vienna, from c.1440; this painting shows the Virgin at the foot of the cross and weeping profusely. Joining the Virgin, though clearly separated from her by space representing temporal distance, are the unidentified donors, a husband and wife who with hands in late medieval positions of prayer seem to be meditating on the scene with the purpose of *feeling* the agony of the event.[38]

The emotionalism of late medieval Christianity owes much, of course, to some rather important theological changes which are too complex to describe fully here.[39] The shift tended to center upon a change from emphasis on the Resurrection to emphasis on the Crucifixion, from Christ's victory toward his sacrificial death upon the cross. Franciscan theology in particular laid great stress upon the close identification of the self with the suffering Christ, but this tendency was ultimately very widespread and is reflected in the vast difference between the static crucifixes of the earlier period and the agonized postures of the representations in art that appear after the twelfth century.[40] The sources of this new *affective theology* have been located in twelfth century theology, particularly through the writings of St. Anselm and the early Cistercians whose emotionalism is well illustrated in the passage quoted from Aelred of Rievaulx above. In art as well as in drama, the new theology provides the basis for understanding forgiveness of one's sins and reconciliation to God in terms of personal identification with the sufferings felt by Christ *as a human*. Thus Walter Hilton wrote of the contemplation of Christ's Passion as follows:

> For it is an opening of the ghostly eye into Christ's manhood. And it may be called the fleshly love of God, as Saint Bernard calleth it, in as mickle as it is set in the fleshly kind of Christ. And it is right good, and a great help in destroying of great sins, and a good way for to come to virtues. And so after to contemplation of the Godhead. For a man shall not come to ghostly delight in contemplation of Christ's Godhead, but he come first in imagination by bitterness and by compassion and by steadfast thinking of his manhood.[41]

This kind of thinking seems particularly to offend the Wycliffite writer, who objects to placing the divine on the same level as the human. By playing, he charges, the master and the servant are confused, and class distinctions are broken down to an intolerable degree. The awful power of God expressed through Christ is thus somehow challenged. But quite normally in orthodox circles of thought during this period Christ was approached precisely on the level of his humanity, which was regarded as an appropriate gateway to proper contemplation of his divinity. Indeed, for a man to come to terms with Christ's divinity, it was often demanded that the approach must first be to his humanity. This position, which on one level was to be sure supported by the theological nominalism that stressed the awful power of God, was of course strongly identified with the Franciscans, who naturally remained under the spell of their founder, St. Francis, himself the recipient of the gift of the stigmata as a sign of his close identification with the sufferings of Christ. It is surely no accident that the Lollards, who objected so loudly to seeing Christ in just such terms, should have targeted the Franciscans as their most bitter opponents.

Dominican theology also came to support the theater in those cases in which drama was turned to the service of good or was presented without evil intent for recreative entertainment. St. Thomas Aquinas defends recreative enjoyment, and tells of "Blessed John the Evangelist" who provided defense of such activity through an analogy; like a bow, "man's mind would break if the tension were never relaxed." Not surprisingly, he insists that pleasure is never to "be sought in indecent or injurious deeds or words."[42] But pleasure itself is not more wicked than sleep, a function that likewise disengages men's reason.[43] Drama is therefore not to be judged evil if it provides recreation without licentiousness, nor are actors themselves members of an illicit vocation. "The occupation of play-actors, the object of which is to cheer the heart of man, is not unlawful in itself; nor are they in a state of sin provided that their playing be moderated, namely that they use no unlawful words or deeds to amuse, and that they do not introduce play into undue matters and seasons."[44] Such a view of plays and players is of course, completely opposed to the insistence upon total seriousness that characterizes *A Tretise of Miraclis Pleyinge*, which implicitly rejects Aquinas' position in favor of the sternest medieval asceticism. The author of the *Tretise* ridicules the idea that "summe recreacioun men moten han, and bettere it is (or lesse yvele) that they han theire recreacioun by pleyinge of miraclis than by pleyinge of other japis." For the writer, "al holinesse is in ful ernest."

The Wycliffite attack on the stage seems to be inspired by widespread popularity of vernacular drama in the late fourteenth and early fifteenth centuries--i.e., the period 1482 to about 1525 when most Lollard writings were produced. John Purvey, the Lollard, thus sneered, "Let us live as our fathers did, and then good enough; for they were well loved of theaters, wrestlers, buckler-players, of dancers and singers. . . ."[45] Yet there is no indication that either the followers of Wyclif or the members of the popular Lollard movement were utterly obsessed by any hatred of the stage,[46] though another document, a poetic attack on the Franciscans' involvement in theatrical presentation, has been attributed to them. The poem, "On the Minorite Friars" from Cotton MS. Cleopatra B.ii, fol. 64[v], attacks Franciscan practices and beliefs on grounds that have been said to be heterodox. Its satire is precisely directed against the scenes of drama or *tableaux vivants* as these were associated with the activities of the friars:

> Of thes frer minours me thenkes moch wonder,
> That waxen are thus hauteyn, that som time weren under.
> Among men of holy chirch, thay maken mochel blonder:
> Nou he that sites us above, make ham sone to sonder.
>> With an O and an I, thay praisen not Seint Poule,
>> Thay lyen on Sein Fraunceys, by my fader soule.
>
> First thay gabben on God that all men may se,
> When thay hangen him on hegh on a grene tre
> With leves and with blossemes that bright are of ble;
> That was never Goddes Son, by my leute.
>> With an O and an I, men wenen that thay wede,
>> To carpe so of clergy that can not thair crede.
>
> Thay have done him on a croys fer up in the skye
> And festned on him wyenges, as he shuld flie;
> This fals feined byleve shal thay soure bye,
> On that lovelich Lord, so forto lye.
>> With an O and an I, one said ful still,

Armachan distroy ham, if it is Goddes will.

Ther comes one out of the skye in a grey goun
As it were an hog-hyerd hyand to toun.
Thay have mo goddes then we, I say by Mahoun,
All men under ham, that ever beres croun.
    With an O and an I, why shuld thay not be shent,
    Ther wantes noght bot a fire that thay nere all
        brent.

Went I forther on my way in that same tide,
Ther I sawe a frere blede in middes of his side,
Bothe in hondes and in fete had he woundes wide,
To serve to that same frer, the pope mot abide.
    With an O and an I, I wonder of thes dedes,
    To se a pope holde a dische whil the frer bledes.

A cart was made al of fire, as it shuld be;
A gray frer I sawe ther-inne, that best liked me.
Wele I wote thay shal be brent, by my leaute--
God graunt me that grace that I may it se.
    With an O and an I, brent be thay all,
    And all that helpes therto faire mot byfall.

Thay preche all of povert, bot that love thay noght,
For gode mete to thair mouthe the toun is thurgh soght.
Wide are thair wonninges and wonderfully wroght;
Murdre and horedome ful dere has it boght.
    With an O and an I, for sixe pens, er thay faile,
    Sle thy fadre and jape thy modre, and thay wil the
        assoile.[47]

In spite of the confusion evident in this poem--its author
does not recognize the nature of the scenes from the life of
St. Francis but mistakes, for example, such tableaux as
those showing the Seraphim as the crucified one appearing to
the saint (stanza 3), the figure of the saint with stigmata
miraculously appearing after his death to Pope Gregory IX
(stanza 5), and the miraculous appearance of the same saint
to his followers at Rivo Torto[48]--it not only verifies the
acting of biblical and saint plays but also suggests a clear
connection with the activities of the Franciscan order.[49]
According to a work written by Wyclif himself, "freris han
taught in Englond the Paternoster in Engliyesh tunge, as men
seyen in the pleye of Yorke. . . ."[50] The poem "On the

Minorite Friars" additionally, like the *Tretise of Miraclis Pleyinge,* appears strongly to imply that the theatrical is simply one more sign of the decadence of the visible Church, which spends its energies in activities that are said to falsify religion rather than to spread the true faith. In spite of evidence that all suspicion could not by the fifteenth century be laid to rest with regard to the appropriateness of playing religious scenes,[51] such activity surely had strong support from the Church and civic leaders in many cities during this period.

As has been recognized,[52] the core of the orthodox defense of drama as reported by the *Tretise* involved the analogy between theatrical presentation and the visual arts: if painting of religious figures and scenes is approved, then the staging of lively depictions of the same in drama must be valued even more highly, for painting by itself "is a deed bok" while dramatic expression gives life. The suspicion with which the iconoclasts viewed the *visible forms* presented on stage therefore provides the most important clue to the aesthetic of medieval vernacular drama. Indeed pictures and plays alike appealed to the sense of sight. Both were inspired, if we read the evidence correctly, by a motive of raising devotion in the viewers.

Some further crucial connections between the visual arts as practiced in the late Middle Ages and the vernacular drama need, however, to be understood. The movement toward verisimilitude in both art and drama has been widely recognized, and we may see some linkage between this phenomenon in artistic practice and the philosophical trends of the period. In Franciscan thought, perception and therefore the senses were of prime importance for the acquiring of knowledge and the apprehending of aesthetic objects.[53] Additionally, the tendency toward nominalism, along with other aspects of mendicant thinking and devotional practice, helped to create a climate in which details from the sacred story *as imagined* could nevertheless function to direct the soul toward the deepest religious experiences. If the religious image is no longer merely the icon through which the devout may make contact with the reality of the person or persons represented,[54] it nevertheless can function as something which existentially brings the soul into tune with the reality of the scene. *Appearances* in such art and/or drama become more important than the *reality* in which the

14

icon participates.[55] The universal and transcendent, previously visualized in forms which tended to eliminate unnecessary specific details, appear often to be put aside in favor of attention to just such details, which to be sure are yet often highly symbolic as in the instance of the symbolism of the architecture denoting the old and new orders in the well known "Friedsam" Annunciation attributed to Hubert van Eyck in the Metropolitan Museum, New York.[56] The new style of handling subjects and details has been directly associated by Erwin Panofsky with nominalism,[57] and hence the following statement by Meyrick H. Carré is worth noting carefully:

> One tendency of the new school of thinkers was the inclination to seek for reality in the individual thing in preference to the universal entity. Associated with this trend there appeared increased emphasis upon intuition or sensory apprehension in knowledge.[58]

Granted such a stance, drama would indeed be likely to be considered superior in some sense to mere painting, which can approximate the forms of life only in a spatial and not in a temporal way. Painting hence might accurately be regarded as less "lively" than theatrical presentation. Additionally, the iconography of religious scenes cannot be simply frozen within such a living art as drama; the details are embued with meaning and placed against a definite background within nature--a technique which stands in perfect opposition to the Byzantine practice of providing depth in front of the picture instead of behind.[59] The assertion of *temporality,* as opposed to the abstract timelessness of earlier Western and Byzantine art, marks late medieval visual presentations of religious scenes as also consistent with the new theological emphasis upon the experience of empathy toward and identification with the humanity of Christ. From the standpoint of such a practical theological position, what better direction could the visual arts take than to overflow into a different form--drama--which in its temporality might more fully express the human feelings and actions of the Savior of men?

The Wycliffite author of *A Tretise of Miraclis Pleyinge,* of course, takes a position which is radically different from the one described above. Though he does not totally condemn the educational function of religious art, he clearly has no sympathy for its role in devotion. With regard to drama and to the devotional function of art, he is in fact a follower of Wyclif, for he maintains a strongly *realist* (as opposed to *nominalist*) position. Images in their devotional function and plays alike provide "sensible" signs that are allegedly lacking in substance and therefore return to the inadequate ways of seeing prevalent in pre-Christian times, Wycliffite thinking insisted.[60] Such devotional aids may prove attractive to the friars, but Wyclif and his followers tended to see the falseness of images, painted glass windows, and lively stage representations, especially when these were regarded as anything more than educational aids--i.e., books for unlettered people. God, who is everywhere present, can hardly be approached more efficiently in an image or through an actor. Hence the concept of the divine *Logos* as potentially communicated through the sense of sight by way of an image as in Byzantine iconophile thinking, is rejected in favor of communication through language alone whenever possible.[61] This shift, which of course foreshadowed the iconoclastic element in the Protestant Reformation, was often set forth all the more radically because of the rigidity and crudity of Wyclif's philosophical position. Humorless and deterministic, the schoolman insisted upon reducing knowledge to exclude anything tentative or imaginative. Gordon Leff notes that his realism was so extreme "that he believed in the self-subsistence of all universal concepts, such as goodness, man and so on, only stopping short of Plato--who had made them autonomous--to locate them eternally in God."[62] Biblical scenes for him were to be understood literally and outside the scheme of time;[63] any attempt to give substance in time to such scenes was to be regarded as vain--an exercise in futility and an affront to the pure understanding of the *Logos*.

Another Wycliffite tract, written by one more antagonistic toward representations in art than the author of the *Tretise of Miraclis Pleyinge,* is the treatise against images and pilgrimages also contained in British Library MS. Add. 24,202. This writer makes a bitter attack upon representations of the Trinity and certain other images which are held to be contrary to scriptural commandment--a disciplinary rather than theological objection. Though he grudgingly is willing to allow men to have a "pore crusifix" since--and here he echoes the orthodox position in defense of such images--Christ had truly become a man, he insists that normally such representations quickly become the occasion for vain displays of jewels and precious metals.[64] With the one exception of the plain crucifix noted above, images are otherwise therefore thoroughly condemned since "the rude puple tristus utterly in thes deade imagis" and thus are encouraged to be lax in their duties to God.[65] The visual arts hence actually provide a distraction which is decidedly seductive in encouraging love of self rather than the performance of charitable acts.[66] Though *A Tretise of Miraclis Pleyinge* is not so restrictive with regard to the kinds of images allowed, it likewise condemns richly adorned devotional images and, of course, applies iconoclastic arguments to the scenes of drama. Here the writer's arguments seem clearly based on Wyclif's realist position. He insists upon seeing "miraclis pleyinge" as "verrey leesing" since the drama presents only "signis withoute dede" for the purpose of seducing viewers out of motives that are as hollowly hypocritical as those of a practiced "lecchour" who "sechith signes of verrey love but no dedis of verrey love." That the *sign* is detached from the "dede" surely is the most serious charge that can be hurled at theatrical representation which presents images and movement that allegedly pretend to be something they are not. In his most serious tone, the author of the *Tretise* writes that "not he that pleyith the wille of God worschipith him, but onely he that doith his wille in deede worschipith him." Therefore, "by siche feinyd miraclis men bygilen hemsilf and dispisen God" in the same manner that Christ's tormentors did when they insisted that he join in their game (see, for example, *Matthew* 26.67-68). The writer identifies their game as the one elsewhere also called "*the bobbid* game,"[67] and specifically associates play-acting with the cruel sport of the torturers "that bobbiden Crist."

As external signs without inner substance, the scenes of drama are regarded by the Wycliffite writer to be lacking in reality; hence they are to be understood as false.[68] For those who regarded the plays highly, however, the signs were on the contrary felt to be practical guides to a proper devotional state of mind. The plays were indeed viewed as useful for confirmation of belief, as in the instance of the priest in *The Hundred Merry Tales* who, when expounding the Creed, advised: "And if you beleve not me, then for more suerte and sufficient auctorite go your way to Coventre and there ye shall se them all playd in Corpus Cristi playe."[69] But principally the plays were devotional, with the scenes informed by a desire to bring to life in an imaginative way precisely those scenes from biblical history or the lives of the saints which were felt to touch most closely the feelings and thoughts of the individual spectators. As signs, the plays are thus highly efficient in that they appeal directly to basic aesthetic experience in a way that spontaneously stimulates enjoyment; through this process, the senses become for the audience the gateway through which the soul may receive enlightenment. In *Dives and Pauper*, a treatise written c.1405-10, we may read that there is crucial religious value in miracles which "arn don principaly for devocioun and honest merthe to teche men to love God the more"--in contrast, of course, to "ribaudye" which takes men away from the proper service of God.[70]

The passage cited immediately above from *Dives and Pauper* is in its entirety, as Kolve has noted, "among contemporary notices of the drama . . . second in length only to the Wycliffite Sermon."[71] In contrast to the Wycliffite work, it provides a strong defense of playing as an expression of mirth, even within the context of Sunday observances. Though there is some nervousness about not only "ribaudye" but also "errour" and "pleyys agens the feith of holy chirche" or its "statys" as well as "good livinge," the speaker, who is Pauper, insists that "Alle other arn defendyd both in haliday and warke day." Specifically approved as "leful and comendable" is the representation "in pleyinge at Cristemesse Heroudis and the thre kingis and other proces of the gospel both in than and at Estryn and in othir times also." Thereupon Dives asks, "Than it semyth be thin speche that in halidayys men mon lefully makyn merthe?" and Pauper responds, "God forbede ellis."[72]

Dives and Pauper does, however, take into account the objection of the early Church to the theater. Following the quoting of Psalm 117.24 ("This is the day that God made; make we now merye and be we glade"), Dives says, "Contra. Sent Austin seith that it were lesse wicke to gon at the plow and at the carte and cardyn and spinnyn in the Sonday than to ledyn dauncis," which are grouped together here with plays. Pauper's response is significant:

18

> Sent Austin spekyth of swyche dauncis and pleyys
> as wern usyd in his time whan Cristene peple was
> muchil medelyd with hethene peple and be old cus-
> tom and example of hethene peple usyd unhonest
> dauncis and pleyys that be eld time wern ordeinyd
> to steryn folc to lecherie and to othir sinnys.
> And so if daunsing and pleyying now on halidayes
> steryn men and wymmen to pride, to lecchery, glo-
> tonye, and slouthe, to over-longe waking on
> nightys and to idilschip on the werkedayes and
> other sinnes, as it is right likly that they done
> in oure dayes, than ar they unleful bothe on the
> haliday and on the werke day, and agens alle
> swyche spak Sent Austin. But agenys honest daun-
> cis and honest pleyys don in dew time and in good
> maner in the haliday spak never Sent Austin.[73]

Hereupon, Dives objects further that the biblical account
demands solemnity and mourning on the Sabbath, but again
Pauper turns the argument aside and proves that, except in
certain seasons, people should experience mirth and engage
in recreation rather than sorrowful exercises on Sundays and
feast days.[74]

But for the Wycliffite writer and the ascetic tradition
the presentation of religious plays is not useful recreation
but instead is "maumetrie"--i.e., the worship of idols, after "Mahomet." The distinctions which had long set pagan
idols apart from Christian images thus are collapsed in a
manner that must have puzzled and angered the average
churchman of the time, though clearly this kind of thinking
was to become dominant in the more radical Protestantism
that insisted upon the suppression of religious images and
of stage actions in the sixteenth and seventeenth centuries.
For the earlier orthodox churchman, however, religious images were indeed normally associated with divine power
which might be available to those who approached them in the
right way.[75] As channels between the worshipper and the
transcendent reality, images since the late Patristic period
had been crucial to Christian devotion. The orthodox view
of the liturgical drama surely drew on the understanding of
the devotional image, though, as we have seen, some changes
in the nature of devotion were introduced in the late Middle Ages which altered the devotional response to both images and vernacular plays. Nevertheless, the bond of emo-

tion that was established between audience and the character represented by the actor was intended to be an authentic religious experience. The orthodox position is exactly stated by the Wycliffite writer: "ofte sithis by siche miraclis pleyinge men and wymmen, seinge the passioun of Crist and of hise seintis, ben movyd to compassion and devocion, wepinge bitere teris, thanne they ben not scoringe of God but worschiping." Durandus had much earlier insisted that pictures move the soul more directly than words,[76] and the Wycliffite writer cites those, as we have seen, who feel that the lively images of drama are even more likely to present an emotional impact on the soul.

But from the point of view of the Wycliffite writer, the playing of scenes, since they are in his opinion false, must substitute *jest* for the *earnestness* with which the realities perceived by a religious person ought to be approached. A play is a *game*, which rearranges the social and cosmic realities according to seemingly arbitrary rules by which the players must abide. Holiness, as we have seen, is "in ful ernest," while *playing* involves even that which will provoke laughter.[77] The *Tretise* insists, following the precedent of St. John Chrysostom, that Christ never laughed,[78] and it would appear that the humorless Wycliffite writer was able to see no excuse whatsoever for levity. Yet, if we are to take the words of the *Tretise* as evidence which is also corroborated from other sources, people ordinarily in fact had by then come to see drama in terms of game. Corroboration for thus understanding the late medieval religious stage hence comes from linguistic evidence as well as from the Wycliffite treatise. Normally, therefore, those who produced and watched the late medieval vernacular plays saw nothing harmful about seeing a play in terms of *play*. Such playing, however, was required to be understood in terms appropriate to the time and not merely to modern theory which is capable of twisting the past to fit modern presuppositions and prejudices. *Playing* is in the vernacular plays something to be displayed--i.e., something to be seen by members of an audience, who are encouraged to engage themselves imaginatively in the scenes that are represented before their eyes. The *purpose* is in the end something more than mere recreation, though the recreative element is not denied. Playing is in fact intended to lead toward the enlightenment of the audience and to its improvement in the life of the spirit. This is possible because, as modern phenomenological study has demonstrated, the play may result in the deconcealment of Being.[79] If the late medieval sponsors of such plays had not also thought thus, they would never have consented to the huge expenditures of money that are recorded for the production of civic drama in such civic centers as York where the Corpus Christi play was presented "especially for the honour and reverence of our Lord Jesus Christ and for the profit of the . . . citizens."[80]

The Manuscript. The Tenison Manuscript (British Library MS. Add. 24,202), which contains *A Tretise of Miraclis Pleyinge,* is a collection of Wycliffite and other writings copied at the beginning of the fifteenth century.[81] Though apparently originating in the Midlands where the Lollard movement was strong, the dialect otherwise does not locate its origin with any greater precision.[82] However, it would seem that the writing could hardly have been done in a region which did not give strong support to civic religious drama, and there is to be sure evidence of such support in the central Midlands (see especially *Two Coventry Corpus Christi Plays,* ed. Hardin Craig, EETS, e.s. 70 [1957]). As noted above, it is not certain even that the entire treatise was indeed the work of a single writer, though for lack of evidence to the contrary we must for the present refer to the author or authors as a single individual. The second part of the *Tretise* has been regarded as the more radical, and speaks quite directly to a friend who shares unorthodox views but supports plays. This friend might even have been someone directly involved with the civic support for such plays in a major civic center such as Coventry. In contrast, the first part of the *Tretise,* though it reflects the concerns of the Wycliffites, seems more within the tradition of anti-theatrical writing inherited from the early Church.

The current edition of the *Tretise* is designed to make it available in a form accessible to students of medieval drama. An attempt has been made to produce a text much more faithful to the original than the somewhat inaccurate editions of Halliwell and Mätzner, which were both subject to the erratic methods of the nineteenth-century copyists who served as intermediaries between manuscript and printer. Nevertheless, because the aim has been also to produce a highly readable text, certain elements of orthography have been regularized. The þ and ȝ have been replaced by modern

21

equivalents, while the letters j, i, y, u, and v have been regularized as much as possible to conform with modern usage. Capital letters have been supplied where appropriate, abbreviations have been silently expanded, and punctuation has been partially modernized though always in a manner consistent with the indications in the manuscript. Some paragraphing has also been added in the interests of readability.

NOTES

[1]Rosemary Woolf, *The English Mystery Plays* (Berkeley and Los Angeles: Univ. of California Press, 1972), p. 85; see *Selections from English Wycliffite Writings*, ed. Anne Hudson (Cambridge: Cambridge Univ. Press, 1978), pp. 83-88, for the Wycliffite treatise against images and pilgrimages.

[2]V. A. Kolve, *The Play Called Corpus Christi* (Stanford: Stanford Univ. Press, 1966), p. 11; for the argument that "this drama had no theory and aimed consciously at no dramatic effects," see Hardin Craig, *English Religious Drama of the Middle Ages* (Oxford: Clarendon Press, 1955), p. 9.

[3]*Altenglische Sprachproben*, ed. Eduard Mätzner (Berlin, 1869), I, Pt. 2, 222.

[4]Harold C. Gardiner, *Mysteries' End*, Yale Studies in English, 103 (New Haven: Yale Univ. Press, 1946), *passim*.

[5]Tertullian, *De Spectaculis*, Loeb Classical Library (Cambridge: Harvard Univ. Press, 1931), pp. 260-61.

[6]Ibid., pp. 274-75.

[7]Ibid., pp. 292-93.

[8]Isidore of Seville, *Etymologiarum*, ed. W. M. Lindsay (Oxford: Clarendon Press, 1911), Vol. II, Book XVIII.xlii.

[9]Mary H. Marshall, "Theatre in the Middle Ages: Evidence from Dictionaries and Glosses," *Symposium*, 4 (1950),

8-9, 39, 375-76.

[10]Ibid., p. 372.

[11]Douglas Percy Bliss, *A History of Wood Engraving* (1928; rpt. London: Spring Books, 1964), p. 53.

[12]E. K. Chambers, *The Mediaeval Stage* (Oxford: Oxford Univ. Press, 1903), II, 98-99.

[13]Ibid., II, 98n.

[14]Ibid.

[15]Karl Young, *The Drama of the Medieval Church* (Oxford: Clarendon Press, 1933), I, 548.

[16]Quoted in Sixten Ringbom, *Icon to Narrative*, Acta Academiae Aboensis, ser. A, 31, No. 2 (Åbo: Åbo Akademi, 1965), p. 16.

[17]Allardyce Nicoll, *Masks, Mimes, and Miracles* (London: George G. Harrap, 1931), p. 146.

[18]J. D. A. Ogilvy, "*Mimi, Scurrae, Histriones*: Entertainers of the Early Middle Ages," *Speculum*, 38 (1963), 608-12.

[19]Richard Axton, *European Drama of the Early Middle Ages* (London: Hutchinson, 1974), p. 19; Chambers, *Mediaeval Stage*, I, 32n.

[20]Nicoll, p. 147.

[21]*Mediaeval Stage*, I, 91.

[22]David Bevington, *Medieval Drama* (Boston: Houghton Mifflin, 1975), p. 9; Young, I, 83.

[23]O. B. Hardison, Jr., *Christian Rite and Christian Drama in the Middle Ages* (Baltimore: Johns Hopkins Press, 1965), pp. 45-77.

[24]For comment on earlier forms, see C. Clifford Flanigan, "The Roman Rite and the Origins of the Liturgical Dra-

ma," *University of Toronto Quarterly*, 43 (1974), 263-84.

[25]Chambers, II, 379-80; Woolf, pp. 29, 349.

[26]Ernst Curtius, *European Literature and the Latin Middle Ages*, trans. Willard R. Trask (1953; rpt. New York: Harper and Row, 1963), pp. 138-44.

[27]*Robert of Brunne's Handlyng Synne*, ed. F. J. Furnivall, EETS, o.s. 119 (1901), p. 155.

[28]Ibid., p. 155. See also the attack against "karolles, wrastlinges, or somour games" in the "cherche, other in chercheyerd" (ibid., p. 283). For another adaptation of the *Manuel des Péchés*, see the identification by Nicholas Davis in his Cambridge University dissertation, "The Playing of Miracles, c. 1350 to the Reformation" (1978), pp. 42-45.

[29]First suggested by Charles Davidson, *Studies in the English Mystery Plays* (1892).

[30]See especially Stanley J. Kahrl, *Traditions of Medieval English Drama* (London: Hutchinson, 1974), pp. 27-52.

[31]Axton, p. 162; Young, II, 539.

[32]R. Davies, *Extracts from the Municipal Records of the City of York during the Reigns of Edward IV, Edward V, and Richard III* (1843); Latin text ed. Alexandra F. Johnston and Margaret (Dorrell) Rogerson, *York*, Records of Early English Drama, 1-2 (Toronto: Univ. Of Toronto Press, 1979), I, 43.

[33]British Library MS. Add. 35,290. The only edition to date is that of Lucy Toulmin Smith, ed., *York Plays* (1885).

[34]See Alexandra F. Johnston, "The Guild of Corpus Christi and the Procession of Corpus Christi in York," *Mediaeval Studies*, 38 (1976), 372-84. On the spirituality which informed the plays, see Clifford Davidson, "Northern Spirituality and Late Medieval Drama of York," *The Spirituality of Western Christendom,* ed. E. Rozanne Elder (Kalamazoo: Cistercian Publications, 1976), pp. 125-51, 205-08, and Theresa Coletti, "Spirituality and Devotional Images: The Staging of the Hegge Cycle," Univ. of Rochester dissertation (1975). Support for seeing civic drama as devotional is given in

such statements as the passage in the *York Memorandum Book A/Y*, fols. 247-247^v, for the year 1422 which specifically identifies devotion and the suppression of vice as purposes of the play; see *York*, ed. Johnston and Rogerson, p. 37. But even direct statements concerning the educational value of the plays, as in the case of the Creed Play, cannot be understood in any positivist way, since the purpose of the tableaux was hardly the mere transmission of information about the facts or mechanics of this world.

[35]Chambers, II, 351; see also the proclamation dated 1532, quoted by F. M. Salter, *Mediaeval Drama in Chester* (Toronto: Univ. of Toronto Press, 1955), pp. 33-34.

[36]See Davidson, "Northern Spirituality," *passim.*

[37]*The Book of Margery Kempe*, ed. Sanford Brown Meech, EETS, o.s. 212 (1940), p. 148. The Franciscan William Melton was critical of Margery Kempe's hysterical weeping, and insisted that she control herself or stay away from a series of sermons he gave at Lynn; see A. B. Emden, *A Biographical Register of the University of Oxford to A.D. 1500* (1958), II, 1258.

[38]Reproductions in Erwin Panofsky, *Early Netherlandish Painting* (Cambridge: Harvard Univ. Press, 1953), II, figs. 322-23; see also commentary in ibid., I, 267. The space which separates the donors from the Passion scene may be said to function very much like that which sets apart dramatic action from audience.

[39]The pioneer theological study is by Gustav Aulén, *Christus Victor*, trans. A. G. Herbert (New York: Macmillan, 1960); the effect on drama is discussed by Sandro Sticca, "Drama and Spirituality in the Middle Ages," *Medievalia et Humanistica*, n.s. 4 (1973), 69-87.

[40]The most important study of the Crucifixion is perhaps that by F. P. Pickering, *Literature and Art in the Middle Ages* (Coral Gables, Florida: Univ. of Miami Press, 1970), pp. 223-307.

[41]Walter Hilton, *The Scale of Perfection*, ed. Evelyn Underhill (London: John M. Watkins, 1948), pp. 80-81. See also Joy M. Russell-Smith, "Walter Hilton and a Tract in De-

fense of the Veneration of Images," *Dominican Studies*, 7 (1954), 194.

[42]*ST*, II, ii, Q. 168, Art. 2; quotations are from the translation by the Fathers of the Church Dominican Province (New York: Benziger, 1947).

[43]*ST*, I, ii, Q. 34, Art. 1, Reply Obj. 1.

[44]*ST*, II, ii, Q. 168, Art. 3.

[45]Quoted by Margeret Deanesly, *The Lollard Bible* (Cambridge: Cambridge Univ. Press, 1920), p. 274.

[46]Hudson, pp. 187-88. It is even possible to suggest that some Lollards may have approved strongly of the didactic (though separated from the devotional) function of playing religious plays, since this would appear to be the case in the instance of the "frend" addressed in Part II of the *Tretise*. Cf. the dissertation by Nicholas Davis, pp. 81-83.

[47]This poem has been edited previously a number of times, first by J. S. Brewer, *Monumenta Franciscana*, Rolls Ser. (London, 1858), I, 606-08, and most recently by Rossell Hope Robbins, *Historical Poems of the XIVth and XVth Centuries* (New York: Columbia Univ. Press, 1959), pp. 163-64. Robbins, however, is most likely mistaken in his notes to the poem when he suggests that it "would seem more appropriate for wall paintings, such as appeared in the large churches the Franciscans built especially for their preaching" (p. 335), than for drama and pageantry, as Wright had suggested in his edition of the poem in *Political Poems and Songs* (London, 1859), pp. 268-70. The most complete discussion of the poem is by Lawrence G. Craddock, "Franciscan Influences on Early English Drama," *Franciscan Studies*, 10 (1950), 399-415. Craddock explains that the dramatic presentations of the friars that are here being attacked were based on the account of the life of St. Francis in the *Legenda Maior* of St. Bonaventure. In line 18 of the poem, *Armachan* is Richard FitzRalph, Archbishop of Armagh in Ireland, who was a fourteenth-century enemy of the Franciscans; he died in 1360, but was remembered by the Wycliffites as a patron who from his heaven seat might intercede against the friars (Craddock, pp. 409-10). On the poem, see also Nicholas Davis' dissertation, pp. 124-31.

[48]Craddock, pp. 408-15.

[49]See David L. Jeffrey, "Franciscan Spirituality and the Rise of Early English Drama," *Mosaic*, 8, No. 4 (1975), 36-40.

[50]John Wyclif, *The English Works*, ed. F. D. Matthew, EETS, o.s. 74 (1880), pp. 429-30. The York Paternoster Play is discussed by Alexandra F. Johnston, "The Plays of the Religious Guilds of York: The Creed Play and the Pater Noster Play," *Speculum*, 50 (1975), 70-80.

[51]See R. W. Hanning, "'You Have Begun a Parlous Pleye': The Nature and Limits of Dramatic Mimesis as a Theme in Four Middle English 'Fall of Lucifer' Cycle Plays," *Comparative Drama*, 7 (1973), 22-50.

[52]Woolf, pp. 86-95; see also Clifford Davidson, *Drama and Art* (Kalamazoo: Medieval Institute, 1977), pp. 12-13.

[53]E. J. M. Spargo, *The Category of the Aesthetic in the Philosophy of St. Bonaventure* (St. Bonaventure, N.Y.: Franciscan Institute, 1953), p. 15.

[54]Religious images (in preference to abstract symbols, such as the Agnus Dei) were approved by the Council of 692 (Canon 82, quoted in translation by Paul J. Alexander, *The Patriarch Nicephorus of Constantinople* [Oxford: Clarendon Press], p. 45), and Eastern theology developed a thoroughgoing defense of their use, particularly in response to iconoclasm. "The honor rendered to the image passes to the prototype," St. Basil had said (quoted by Gerhart B. Ladner, "The Concept of the Image in the Greek Fathers and the Byzantine Iconoclastic Controversy," *Dumbarton Oaks Papers*, 7 [1953], 3). On the implications of the devotional image, see especially Coletti, pp. 31-100.

[55]See Clifford Davidson, "The Realism of the York Realist and the York *Passion*," *Speculum*, 50 (1975), 273-83.

[56]Panofsky, II, fig. 152; see commentary, ibid., I, 133f.

[57]Ibid., I, 35.

[58]Meyrick H. Carré, *Realists and Nominalists* (Oxford, 1946), p. 145. The subject of the changed view of things is,

of course, a complicated one; see, for example, Gordon Leff, *The Dissolution of the Medieval Outlook* (New York: Harper and Row, 1976).

[59]Gervase Mathew, *Byzantine Aesthetics* (New York: Viking Press, 1964), p. 31.

[60]John Wyclif, *Tractatus de Ecclesia,* ed. Johann Loserth (London, 1886), p. 459; attention is called to this passage by John Phillips, *The Reformation of Images* (Berkeley and Los Angeles: Univ. of California Press, 1973), p. 31.

[61]Ibid., pp. 31-33; Kolve, pp. 21-22; cf. Ernst Kitzinger, "The Cult of Images in the Age before Iconoclasm," *Dumbarton Oaks Papers*, 8 (1954), 104, and Ladner, *passim.*

[62]Gordon Leff, *Heresy in the Later Middle Ages* (New York: Barnes and Noble, 1967), II, 501.

[63]Ibid., II, 511.

[64]Hudson, p. 83.

[65]Ibid., p. 87.

[66]Phillips, p. 31; see also G. R. Owst, *Literature and Pulpit in Medieval England,* 2nd ed. (Oxford: Blackwell, 1961), pp. 143-45, but the most important survey of the Wycliffite attitude toward images is contained in J. A. F. Thomson, *The Later Lollards* (Oxford: Oxford Univ. Press, 1965).

[67]It is also called Hot Cockles, and is described in an account in Bodleian MS. 649, fol. 82, of c.1420; the description as quoted by Owst, p. 510, is included in the critical notes, below.

[68]Kolve, p. 22; for an opposing aesthetic position, see especially David L. Jeffrey, *The Early English Lyric and Franciscan Spirituality* (Lincoln: Univ. of Nebraska Press, 1975), pp. 91ff.

[69]*Shakespeare's Jest Book: C. Mery Tales,* ed. H. Oesterley (London, 1866), p. 100.

[70]*Dives and Pauper,* ed. Priscilla Heath Barnum, EETS,

o.s. 275 (1976), I, 293. See also Kolve, pp. 132-33, who re-
prints Pynson's text.

[71]Kolve, p. 131.

[72]*Dives and Pauper*, p. 293.

[73]Ibid., p. 294.

[74]Ibid., pp. 294-95.

[75]See the important article by Richard C. Trexler,
"Florentine Religious Experience: The Sacred Image," *Studies
in the Renaissance*, 19 (1972), 7-41.

[76]*Rationale de divinis offiis* (Naples, 1859), p. 24, as
cited by Woolf, p. 90.

[77]On *play* and *drama*, see especially Kolve, pp. 8-32; cf.
Curtius, pp. 417ff. Needless to say, Kolve's understanding
of the concept of *game* requires careful attention, especially
since his analysis does not always distinguish between medieval conceptions and controversial modern theories. Kolve's
study is, of course, seminal, since many earlier writers on
the medieval drama demonstrated no understanding of the connection between *play* and *drama* whatsoever; see, for example,
George R. Coffman, "The Miracle Play in England--Nomencla-
ture," *PMLA*, 31 (1916), 456-61.

[78]Curtius, p. 420; Kolve (p. 126) additionally cites
the *Cursor Mundi*:
> that thris he wep we find i-nogh,
> Bot we find never quar he logh.

[79]H.-G. Gadamer, *Truth and Method* (New York: Seabury,
1975), pp. 91-119; Martin Heidegger, "The Origin of a Work of
Art," in *Poetry, Language, Thought*, trans. Albert Hofstadter
(New York: Harper and Row, 1971), pp. 17-87.

[80]*York*, ed. Johnston and Rogerson, II, 713.

[81]*Catalogue of Additions to the Manuscripts in the British Museum*, II (1877), 22. The first item in the manuscript is an attack on "The bischopes othe that he sweris
to the pope" (fols. 1-13^V), followed by *A Tretise of Mira-*

clis Pleyinge (fols. 14-21). The items which follow in the
manuscript are: a treatise against dicing (fols. 21-24),
against the showing of relics for profit (fols. 24-24^V), an
epistle to a lady on knowledge of the soul (fols. 25-26), *A
Tretise of Imagys* (fols. 26-28^V), *A Tretise of Pristis* (fols.
28^V-29), *Of Weddid Men and ther Wivis and Ther Childere*
(fols. 29-34, a treatise on tithes and offerings (fols. 34-
35^V), *The Seven Sacramentis* by John Gaytrigg (fols. 35^V-36),
The Sevene Vertues by Gaytrigg (fol. 36^V, incomplete), and a
treatise (fragment) against religious orders (fols. 37-60^V).
The manuscript, from the library of Archbishop Tenison and
formerly at St. Martin-in-the-Fields, London, was purchased
by the British Museum in 1861.

[82]See Davis, p. 83.

SELECTED BIBLIOGRAPHY

Manuscript:

Catalogue of Additions to Manuscripts in the British Museum,
II (London, 1877).

Davis, Nicholas M. "The Playing of Miracles, c.1350 to the
Reformation." Diss., Cambridge University, 1978.

Hudson, Anne. *English Wycliffite Writings*. Cambridge: Cambridge University Press, 1978.

Editions:

Halliwell, J. O., and Thomas Wright. *Relique Antique*. London, 1841.

Halliwell, J. O. *The English Drama and Stage Under the Tudor
and Stuart Princes 1543-1664*. 1869; rpt. New York:
Russell and Russell, n.d.

Mätzner, Eduard. *Altenglische Sprachproben*. Berlin, 1869.
Vol. I, Pt. 2.

Hudson, Anne. *English Wycliffite Writings*. Cambridge: Cambridge University Press, 1978. (Incomplete text.)

Studies:

Chambers, E. K. *The Mediaeval Stage*. Oxford: Oxford University Press, 1903. 2 vols.

Coletti, Theresa. "Spirituality and Devotional Images: The
Staging of the Hegge Cycle." Diss., University of
Rochester, 1975.

Craddock, Lawrence G. "Franciscan Influences on Early English Drama," *Franciscan Studies*, 10 (1950), 399-
415.

Davidson, Clifford. *Drama and Art: An Introduction to the Use of Evidence from the Visual Arts for the Study of Early Drama*. Kalamazoo: Medieval Institute, 1977.

_____. "Northern Spirituality and Late Medieval Drama in York," *The Spirituality of Western Christendom*, ed. E. Rozanne Elder. Kalamazoo: Cistercian Publications, 1976. Pp. 125-51, 205ff.

Davis, Nicholas M. "The Playing of Miracles, c.1350 to the Reformation." Diss., Cambridge University, 1978.

Gardiner, Harold C. *Mysteries' End*. New Haven: Yale University Press, 1946.

Jeffrey, David L. "Franciscan Spirituality and the Rise of Early English Drama," *Mosaic*, 8, No. 4 (1975), 17-46.

Kolve, V. A. *The Play Called Corpus Christi*. Stanford: Stanford University Press, 1966.

Owst, G. R. *Literature and Pulpit in Medieval England,* 2nd ed. Oxford: Blackwell, 1961.

Woolf, Rosemary. *The English Mystery Plays*. Berkeley and Los Angeles: University of California Press, 1972.

A TRETISE OF MIRACLIS PLEYINGE

34

f. 14   Here biginnis a tretise of miraclis pleyinge

Knowe yee, cristen men, that as Crist, God and
man, is bothe weye, trewth, and lif, as seith the
gospel of Jon--weye to the erringe, trewthe to the
unknowing and douting, lif to the styinge to hevene
5   and weryinge--so Crist dude no thinge to us but
efectuely in weye of mercy, in treuthe of ritwesnes,
and in lif of yilding everlastinge joye for oure
contunuely morning and sorwinge in this valey of
teeres. Miraclis, therfore, that Crist dude heere in
10   erthe outher in himsilf outher in hise seintis weren
so efectuel and in ernest done that to sinful men
that erren they broughten forgivenesse of sinne,
settinge hem in the weye of right bileve; to doutouse men not stedefast they broughten in kunning to
15   betere plesen God, and verry hope in God to been
stedefast in him; and to the wery of the weye of
God, for the grette penaunce and suffraunce of the
tribulacioun that men moten have therinne, they
broughten in love of brynninge charite to the whiche
20'   alle thing is light, yhe to suffere dethe, the whiche
men most dreden, for the everlastinge lif and joye
that men most loven and disiren of the whiche thing
verry hope puttith awey all werinesse heere in the
weye of God.

25   Thanne, sithen miraclis of Crist and of hise
seintis weren thus ef[f]ectuel, as by oure bileve we
ben in certein, no man shulde usen in bourde and
pleye the miraclis and werkis that Crist so ernyst-
fully wroughte to oure helthe. For whoevere so
30   doth, he errith in the byleve, reversith Crist, and
scornyth God. He errith in the bileve, for in that
he takith the most precious werkis of God in pley
and bourde, and so takith his name in idil and so
misusith oure byleve. A, Lord, sithen an erthely
35   servaunt dar not takun in pley and in bourde that
that h[is] erthely lord takith in ernest, myche more
we shulden not maken oure pleye and bourde of tho
miraclis and werkis that God so ernestfully wrought

35

to us. For sothely whan we so doun, drede to sinne
40 is takun awey, as a servaunt, whan he bourdith with
his maister, leesith his drede to offendyn him,
namely whanne he bourdith with his maister in that
that his maister takith in ernest. And right as a
nail smiten in holdith two thingis togidere, so
45 drede smiten to Godward holdith and susteineth oure
bileve to him.

Therfore right as pleyinge and bourdinge of the
most ernestful werkis of God takith aweye the drede
of God that men shulden han in the same, so it tak-
50 ith awey oure bileve and so oure most helpe of oure
savac[i]oun. And sith taking awey of oure bileve is
more veniaunce taking than sodeyn taking awey of oure
bodily lif, and whanne we takun in bourde and pley
the most ernestful werkis of God as ben hise mira-
55 clis, God takith awey fro us his grace of mekenesse,
drede, reverence and of oure bileve; thanne, whanne
we pleyin his miraclis as men don nowe on dayes, God
takith more veniaunce on us than a lord that sodayn-
ly sleeth his servaunt for he pleyide to homely with
60 him. And right as that lord thanne in dede seith to
f. 14ᵛ his servaunt, "Pley not with me but pley with thy
pere," so whanne we takun in pley and in bourde the
miraclis of God, he, fro us takinge his grace, seith
more ernestfully to us than the forseid lord, "Pley
65 not with me but pley with thy pere."

Therfore siche miraclis pleyinge reversith
Crist. Firste in taking to pley that that he toke
into most ernest. The secound in taking to miraclis of oure fleyss, of oure lustis, and of oure
70 five wittis that that God tooc to the bringing in
of his bitter deth and to teching of penaunse doinge,
and to fleyinge of feding of oure wittis and to mor-
tifying of hem. And therfore it is that seintis
myche noten that of Cristis lawying we reden never
75 in holy writt, but of his myche penaunse, teris, and
scheding of blod, doying us to witen therby that
alle oure doing heere shulde ben in penaunce, in
disciplining of oure fleyssh, and in penaunce of ad-
versite. And therfore alle the werkis that we don
80 [that] ben out of alle thes thre utturly reversen
Cristis werkis. And therfore seith Seint Poul

[th]at "Yif yee been out of discipline of the whiche
alle gode men ben maad perceneris, thanne avoutreris yee ben and not sones of God." And sith
85 miraclis pleynge reversen penaunce doying as they in
greet liking ben don and to grete liking ben cast
biforn, there as penaunce is in gret mourning of
hert and to greet mourning is ordeinyd biforne.

It also reversith dissipline, for in verry dis-
90 cipline the verry vois of oure maister Crist is herd
as a scoler herith the vois of his maister, and the
yerd of God in the hond of Crist is seyn, in the
whiche sight alle oure othere thre wittis for drede
tremblyn and quaken as a childe tremblith seing the
95 yerde of his maister. And the thridde in verry dissipline is verry turning awey and forgeting of alle
tho thingis that Crist hatith and turnyde himsilf
awey heere as a childe undir dissipline of his maister turnith him awey fro alle thingis that his mais-
100 ter hath forbedun him, and forgetith hem for the
greet minde that he hath to doun his maistris
wille.

And for thes thre writith Seint Petur, seyinge,
"Be yee mekid undur the mighty hond of God that he
105 henhaunce you in the time of visiting, all youre
bisinesse throwinge in him." That is, "be yee
mekid," that is to Crist, heringe his voice by verry obeschaunce to his hestis; and "undur the mighty
hond of God," seeing evere more his yird to chas-
110 tisen us in his hond yif we waxen wantown or idil,
bethenking us, seith Seint Petre, that "hidous and
ferful it is to fallen into the hondis of God on
live." For right as most joye it is to steyen up
into the hond of the mercy of God, so it is most
115 hidous and ferful to fallen into the hondis of the
wrathe of God. Therfore mekely drede we him heere
everemore seyng and thenkinge his yerde overe oure
f. 15 hevyd, and thanne he shal enhauncyn us elliswhere in
time of his graceous visiting. So that alle oure
120 bisinesse we throwyn in him, that is, that alle
othere erthely werkis we don not b[u]t to don his
gostly werkis, more frely and spedely and more
plesauntly to him tristing, that to him is cure
over us, that is, yif we don to him that that is in

37

125 oure power he schal mervelousely don to us that
that is in his power, bothe in dylivering us fro
alle perilis and in giving us graciously al that
us nedith or willen axen of him.

And sithen no man may serven two lordis to-
130 gydere, as seith Crist in his gospel, no man may
heren at onys efectuely the voice of oure maister
Crist and of his owne lustis. And sithen miraclis
pleyinge is of the lustis of the fleyssh and mirthe
of the body, no man may efectuely heeren hem and the
135 voice of Crist at onys, as the voice of Crist and
the voice of the fleysh ben of two contrarious
lordis. And so miraclis pleying reversith discipline, for as seith Seint Poul, *"Eche forsothe discipline in the time that is now is not a joye but a*
140 *mourninge."* Also sithen it makith to se veine
sightis of degyse, aray of men and wymmen by yvil
continaunse, either stiring othere to leccherie and
of debatis as aftir most bodily mirthe comen moste
debatis, as siche mirthe more undisposith a man to
145 paciencie and ablith to glotonye and to othere
vicis, wherfore it suffrith not a man to beholden
enterly the yerde of God over his heved, but makith
to thenken on alle siche thingis that Crist by the
dedis of his passion badde us to forgeten. Wher-
150 fore siche miraclis pleyinge, bothe in penaunce
doying, in verry discipline, and in pacience re-
versyn Cristis hestis and his dedis.

Also, siche miraclis pleying is scorning of
God, for right as ernestful leving of that that God
155 biddith is dispising of God, as dide Pharao so
bourdfully taking Goddis biddings or wordis or
werkis in scorning of him, as diden the Jewis that
bobbiden Crist, thanne, sithen thes miraclis pleyeris taken in bourde the ernestful werkis of God,
160 no doute that ne they scornen God as diden the
Jewis that bobbiden Crist, for they lowen at his
passioun as these lowyn and japen of the miraclis of
God. Therfore as they scorneden Crist, so theese
scorne God. And right as Pharao, wrooth to do that
165 God bad him, dispiside God, so these miraclis pleyeris and maintenours leevinge plesingly to do that
God biddith hem scornen God. He forsothe hath beden

38

us alle to halowyn his name, giving drede and reverence in alle mind of his werkis withoute ony pleying or japinge, as al holinesse is in ful ernest. Men thanne pleyinge the name of Goddis miraclis as plesingly, they leeve to do that God biddith hem so they scornen his name and so scornyn him.

But here agenus they seyen that they pleyen these miraclis in the worschip of God and so diden not thes Jewis that bobbiden Crist.

Also ofte sithis by siche miraclis pleyinge ben men convertid to gode livinge, as men and wymmen seing in miraclis pleyinge that the devul by ther aray, by the whiche they moven eche on othere to leccherie and to pride, makith hem his servauntis to bringen hemsilf and many othere to helle, and to han fer more vilenye herafter by ther proude aray heere than they han worschipe heere, and seeinge ferthermore that al this worldly being heere is but vanite, for a while as is miraclis pleying, wherthoru they leeven pride and taken to hem afterward the meke conversacioun of Crist and of hise seintis. And so miraclis pleying turneth men to the bileve and not pervertith.

Also ofte sithis by siche miraclis pleyinge men and wymmen, seinge the passioun of Crist and of hise seintis, ben movyd to compassion and devocion, wepinge bitere teris, thanne they ben not scorninge of God but worschiping.

Also prophitable to men and to the worschipe of God it is to fulfillun and sechen alle the menes by the whiche men mowen leeve sinne and drawen hem to vertues and sithen as ther ben men that only by ernestful doinge wilen be convertid to God, so ther been othere men that wilen not be convertid to God but by gamen and pley. And now on dayes men ben not convertid by the ernestful doing of God ne of men. Thanne now it is time and skilful to assayen to convertyn the puple by pley and gamen as by miraclis pleyinge and other maner mirthis.

Also summe recreacioun men moten han, and bet-

tere it is (or lesse yvele) that they han theire
recreacioun by pleyinge of miraclis than by pleyinge
210   of other japis.

        Also sithen it is leveful to han the miraclis
of God peintid, why is not as wel leveful to han the
miraclis of God pleyed, sithen men mowen bettere
reden the wille of God and his mervelous werkis in
215   the pleyinge of hem than in the peintinge? And
betere they ben holden in mennus minde and oftere
rehersid by the pleyinge of hem than by the
peintinge, for this is a deed bok, the tother a
qu[i]ck.

220   [1.] To the first resoun we answeryn seying
that siche miraclis pleyinge is not to the worschipe
of God, for they ben don more to ben seen of the
worlde and to plesyn to the world thanne to ben seen
of God or to plesyn to him as Crist never ensaumplide
225   hem but onely hethene men that evere more dishon-
ouren God, seyinge that to the worschipe of God that
is to the most veleynye of him. Therfore as the
wickidnesse of the misbileve of hethene men lyith to
themsilf, whanne they seyn that the worshiping of
230   theire maumetrie is to the worschipe of God, so
mennus lecherye now on dayes to han ther owne lustus
lieth to hemself whanne they seyn that suche miracles pleying is to the worschip of God. For Crist
seith that folc of avoutrie sechen siche singnys as
235   a lecchour sechith signes of verrey love but no
dedis of verrey love. So sithen thise miraclis pleyinge ben onely singnis, love withoute dedis, they
ben not onely contrarious to the worschipe of God--
that is, bothe in signe and in dede--but also they
240   ben ginnys of the devuel to cacchen men to byleve of
Anticrist, as wordis of love withoute verrey dede ben
ginnys of the lecchour to cacchen felawchipe to
fulfillinge of his leccherie. Bothe for these miraclis pleyinge been verrey leesing as they ben
245   signis withoute dede and for they been verrey idilnesse, as they taken the miraclis of God in idil af-
tur theire owne lust. And certis idilnesse and
leesing been the most ginnys of the dyvul to drawen
men to the byleve of Anticrist. And therfore to
f. 16   pristis it is uttirly forbedyn not onely to been

miracle pleyere, but also to heren or to seen miraclis pleyinge lest he that shulde been the ginne of
God to cacchen men and to holden men in the bileve
of Crist, they ben maad agenward by ypocrisie,
255 the gin of the devel to cacchen men to the bileve of
Anticrist. Therfore right as a man sweringe in idil
by the names of God and seyinge that in that he worschipith God and dispisith the devil, verrily lyinge
doth the reverse; so miraclis pleyers, as they ben
260 doers of idilnesse, seyinge that they don it to the
worschip of God, verreyly liyn. For, as seith the
gospel, "Not he that seith, 'Lord, Lord,' schal come
to blisse of hevene, but he that doth the wille of
the fadir of hevene schal come to his kindam." So
265 myche more not he that pleyith the wille of God worschipith him, but onely he that doith his wille in
deede worschipith him. Right therfore as men by
feinyd tokenes bygilen and in dede dispisen ther
neighboris, so by siche feinyd miraclis men bygilen
270 hemsilf and dispisen God, as the tormentours that
bobbiden Crist.

[2.] And as anentis the secound reson, we
seyen that right as a vertuous deede is othere
while occasioun of yvel, as was the passioun of
275 Crist to the Jewis, but not occasioun given but
taken of hem, so yvele dedis ben occasioun of gode
dedis othere while, as was the sinne of Adam occasioun of the coming of Crist, but not occasion
given of the sinne but occasion takun of the grete
280 mercy of God. The same wise miraclis pleyinge, al
be it that it be sinne, is othere while occasion of
converting of men, but as it is sinne it is fer
more occasion of perverting of men, not onely of oon
singuler persone but of al an hool comynte, as it
285 makith al a puple to ben ocupied in vein agenus this
heeste of the Psauter book that seith to alle men
and namely to pristis that eche day reden it in ther
servise, "*Turne awey min eyen that they se not vanitees,*" and efte "*Lord, thou hati*[*dest*] *alle waitinge*
290 *vanitees.*" How thanne may a prist pleyn in entirlodies or give himsilf to the sight of hem sithen it
is forbeden him so expresse by the forseide heste of
God, namely sithen he cursith eche day in his service alle tho that bowen awey fro the hestis of God.

41

295 But, alas, more harme is, pristis now on dayes most
shrewyn hemsilf al day as a jay that al day crieth,
"Watte shrewe!" shrewinge himsilf. Therfore miraclis pleyinge, sithen it is agenus the heest of God
that biddith that thou shalt not take Goddis name
300 in idil, it is agenus oure bileve and so it may not
given occacioun of turninge men to the bileve but of
perverting. And therfore many men wenen that ther
is no helle of everelastinge peine, but that God
doth but thretith us, not to do it in dede, as ben
305 pleyinge of miraclis in signe and not in dede. Therfore siche miraclis pleying not onely pervertith
oure bileve but oure verry hope in God, by the
whiche seintis hopiden that that the more they ab-
steneden hem fro siche pleyes, the more mede they
310 shulden have of God; and therfore the holy Sara,
the doughter of Raguel, hopinge heie mede of God,
f. 16ᵛ seith, "Lord, thou woost that nevere I coveytide
man, and clene I have kept my sowle fro all lustis,
nevere with pleyeris I mingid me mysilfe person,"
315 and by this trwe confessioun to God, as she hopide,
so sche hadde hir preyeris herd and grete mede of
God. And sithen a yonge womman of the Olde Testament for keping of hir bodily vertue of chastite and
for to worthily take the sacrament of matrimonye
320 whanne hir time shulde come, abstenyde hir fro al
maner idil pleying and fro al cumpany of idil pleyeris, myche more a prist of the Newe Testament, that
is passid the time of childehod and that not onely
shulde kepe chastite but alle othere vertues, ne
325 onely ministren the sacrament of mat[ri]monye but
alle othere sacramentis and namely sithen him owith
to ministre to alle the puple the precious body of
Crist, awghte to abstene him fro al idil pleying
bothe of miraclis and ellis. For certis, sithen the
330 quen of Saba, as seith Crist in the gospel, schal
dampne the Jewis that wolden not reseive the wisdom
of Crist, myche more this holy womman Sara at the
day of dom schal dampnen the pristis of the Newe
Testament that givis heem to pleyes, reversen her
335 holy maners aprovyd by God and al holy chirche;
therfore sore aughten pristis to be aschamyd that
reversen this gode holy womman and the precious body
of Crist that they treytyn in ther hondis, the
whiche body never gaf him to pley but to alle siche

340 thing as is most contrarious to pley, as is penaunce
and suffring of persecution.

And so thes miraclis pleyinge not onely reversith feith and hope but verry charite by the
whiche a man shulde weilen for his owne sinne and for
345 his neieburs, and namely pristis for it withdrawith
not onely oon persone but alle the puple fro dedis
of charite and of penaunce into dedis of lustis and
likingis and of feding of houre wittis. So thanne
thes men that seyen, "Pley we a pley of Anticrist
350 and of the Day of Dome that sum man may be convertid therby," fallen into the herisie of hem that,
reversing the aposteyl, seiden, "Do we yvel thingis,
that ther comyn gode thingis," of whom, as seith the
aposteyl, "dampning is rightwise."

355 [3.] By this we answeren to the thridde resoun
seyinge that siche miraclis pleyinge giveth noon occasioun of werrey wepinge and medeful, but the weping
that fallith to men and wymmen by the sighte of
siche miraclis pleyinge, as they ben not principaly
360 for theire oune sinnes ne of theire gode feith with-
inneforthe, but more of theire sight withouteforth
is not alowable byfore God but more reprowable. For
sithen Crist himsilf reprovyde the wymmen that wepten upon him in his passioun, myche more they ben
365 reprovable that wepen for the pley of Cristis passioun, leevinge to wepen for the sinnes of hemsilf
and of theire children, as Crist bad the wymmen that
wepten on him.

[4.] And by this we answeren to the furthe re-
f. 17 soun, seyinge that no man may be convertid to God but
onely by the ernestful doyinge of God and by noon
vein pleying, for that that the Word of God worchith
not ne his sacramentis, how shulde pleyinge worchen
that is of no vertue but ful of defaute? Therfore
375 right as the weping that men wepen ofte in siche
pley comunely is fals wittnessenge that they lovyn
more the liking of theire body and of prosperite of
the world than likinge in God and prosperite of vertu in the soule, and, therfore, having more compas-
380 sion of peine than of sinne, they falsly wepyn for
lakkinge of bodily prosperite more than for lakking

43

of gostly, as don dampnyd men in helle. Right so,
ofte sithis the convertinge that men semen to ben
convertid by siche pleyinge is but feinyd holinesse,
385   worse than is othere sinne biforehande. For yif he
were werrily convertid, he shulde haten to seen
alle siche vanite, as biddith the hestis of God, al
be it that of siche pley he take occasion by the
grace of God to fle sinne and to folowe vertu. And
390   yif men seyn heere that yif this pleyinge of miraclis were sinne, why while God converten men by the
occasion of siche pleyinge, heereto we seyen that
God doith so for to comenden his mersy to us, that
we thenken enterly hou good God is to us, that whil
395   we ben thenkinge agenus him, doing idilnesse and
withseyinge him, he thenkith upon us good, and
sendinge us his grace to fleen alle siche vanite.
And for ther shulde no thinge be more swete to us
than siche maner mercy of God, the Psauter book
400   clepith that mercy "blessinge of swetnesse" where
he seith, "*Thou cam bifore him in blessinges of
swetnesse*"--the whiche swetnesse, al be it that
it be likinge to the spirit, it is while we ben
here ful travelous to the body, whan it is verry
405   as the flesche and the spirit ben contrarious;
therfore this swetnesse in God wil not been verely
had while a man is ocuped in seinge of pleyis.
Therfore the pristis that seyn hemsilf holy and
bysien hem aboute siche pleyis ben verry ypocritis
410   and lieris.

[5.] And herby we answeren to the fifte resoun
seyinge that verry recreacion is leeveful, ocupyinge
in lasse werkis, to more ardently worschen grettere
werkis. And therfore siche miraclis pleyinge ne
415   the sight of hem is no verrey recreasion but fals
and worldly, as provyn the dedis of the fautours of
siche pleyis that yit nevere tastiden verely swetnesse in God, traveilinge so myche therinne that
their body wolde not sofisen to beren siche a tra-
420   veile of the spirite, but as man goith fro vertue
into vertue, so they gon fro lust into lust that
they more stedefastly dwellen in hem. And therfore
as this feinyd recreacioun of pleyinge of miraclis
is fals equite, so it is double shrewidnesse, worse
425   than thou[gh] they pleyiden pure vaniteis. For now

the puple giveth credence to many mengid leesingis
for othere mengid trewthis and maken wenen to been
gode that is ful yvel, and so ofte sithis lasse
f. 17ᵛ yvele it were to pleyin rebaudye than to pleyin
430 siche miriclis. And yif men axen what recreacioun
men shulden have on the haliday after theire holy
contemplacioun in the chirche, we seyen to hem two
thingis--oon, that yif he hadde verily ocupiede him
in contemplac[i]oun byforn, neither he wolde aske
435 that question ne han wille to se vanite; another we
seyn, that his recreacioun shulde ben in the werkis
of mercy to his neiebore and in diliting him in alle
good comunicacion with his neibore, as biforn he
dilitid him in God, and in alle othere nedeful
440 werkis that reson and kinde axen.

[6.] And to the laste reson we seyn that
peinture, yif it be verry withoute menging of lesingis and not to curious, to myche fedinge mennus
wittis, and not occasion of maumetrie to the puple,
445 they ben but as nakyd lettris to a clerk to riden
the treuthe. But so ben not miraclis pleyinge that
ben made more to deliten men bodily than to ben
bokis to lewid men. And therfore yif they ben quike
bookis, they ben quike bookis to shrewidenesse more
450 than to godenesse. Gode men therfore seinge ther
time to schort to ocupien hem in gode ernest werkis,
and seinge the day of ther rekeninge neighen faste,
and unknowing whan they schal go hennys, fleen alle
siche idilnessis, hyinge that they weren with her
455 spouse Crist in the blisse of hevene.

An half frynde tariere to soule helthe, redy to
excusen the yvil and hard of bileve, with Thomas of
Inde, seith that he wil not leevyn the forseid sentense of miraclis pleyinge but and men schewen it
460 him by holy writt opynly and by oure bileve. Wherfore that his half frenschip may be turnyd to the
hoole, we preyen him to beholden first in the sec-
onde maundement of God that seith, "Thou shalt not
take Goddis name in idil," and sithen the mervelous
465 werkis of God ben his name, as the gode werkis of a
craftesman been his name, than in this hest of God
is forbeden to takun the mervelouse werkis of God
in idil. And how mowen they be more takyn in idil

45

than whanne they ben maad mennus japinge stikke, as
470 when they ben playid of japeris? And sithen ernest-
ly God dide hem to us, so take we hem of him; ellis
fo[r]sothe we taken hem in vein. Loke thanne,
frend, yif thy byleve tellith that God dide his
miraclis to us for we shulden pleyn hem--and ye
475 trowe it seith to the, "Nay, but for thou schuldist
more dredyn him and lovyn him." And certis greet
drede and gret effectuel loove suffrith no pleyinge
nor japing with him. Thanne sithen miraclis pleyinge reversith the wille of God and the ende for the
480 whiche he wrought miraclis to us, no doute but that
miraclis pleyinge is verre taking of Goddis name in
idil.

And yif this suffisith not to thee, al be it
that it shulde suffisen to an hethene man that ther-
485 fore wil not pleyin the werkis of his mawmete, I
preye thee rede enterly in the book of lif that is
Crist Jhesus and if thou mayst finden in him that
f. 18 he evere exsaumplide that men shulden pleye miraclis, but alwey the revers and oure byleve cursith
490 that hadden or lassen over that Crist exsaumplide
us to don. Hou thanne darst thou holden with miraclis pleyinge sithen alle the werkis of Crist re-
versiden hem, and in none of his werkis they ben
groundyd?--namely, sithen thou seyst thyselven that
495 thou wolt nothing leven but that may be schewid of
oure bileve, and sithen in thing that is acording
with the fleyssh and to the liking of it, as is
miraclis pleyinge, thou wilt nothing don agenus it,
but yif it be schewid of oure bileve; myche more in
500 thing that is with the spirit, and alwey exsawmplid
in the lif of Crist and so fully writen in the
booke of lif, as is leving of miraclis pleyinge and
of all japing, thou shuldest not holden agenys it,
but if it mighte ben schewid agens the bileve,
505 sithen in al thing that is dowtous men schulden
holden with the partye that is more favowrable to
the spirit and more exsawmpplid in the lif of
Crist. And so as eche sinne distruyith himsilf and
eche falshed, so thy answere distruyith himsilfe and
510 therby thou mayst wel witen that it is not trewe,
but verre unkindenesse; for if thou haddist hadde a
fadir that hadde suffred a dispitouse deth to geten

46

thee thin heritage, and thou therafter woldest so
lightly bern it to make therof a pley to the and to
515 alle the puple, no dowte but that alle gode men
wolden demyn the unkinde, miche more God and alle
his seintes demyen alle tho cristen men unkinde that
pleyen or favouren the pley of the deth or of the
miracles of the most kinde fadir Crist that diede
520 and wroughte miraclis to bringen men to the everelastande heretage of hevene.

But peraventure heere thou seist that of pleyinge of miraclis be sinne, never the latere it is
but litil sinne. But herfore, dere frend, knowe yee
525 that eche sinne, be it never so litil, if it be
maintenyd and prechid as gode and profitable, is
deadely sinne; and therfore seith the prophite, *"Wo
to hem that seyen gode, yvel, and yvel, good."* And
therfore the wise man dampneth hem that gladen whan
530 they don yvel; and therfore alle seintis seyen that
mannische it is to fallen, but develiche it is to
abiden stille therinne. Therfore, sithen thes miraclis pleyinge is sinne, as thou knowlechist, and is
stedefastly meintenyd, and also men deliten hem
535 therinne, no dowte but that it is deadly sinne and
dampnable, develiche not mannisch. Lord, sithen
Adam and Eve and al mankinde weren dampnyd out of
paradise not onely for eting of the appul, but more
for the excusing therof, myche more pleyinge of
540 miraclis not onely excusid but stedefastly meintenyd is dampnable and deadly, namely sithen it not
onely pervertith oon man but al a puple that they
seyen good, yvel, and yvel, gode.

And if this wil not suffise thee, al be it
545 that it shulde suffisen to eche cristen man (that
nothing schulde donn oute of the teching that
Crist taughte), tac hide to the dedis that God
hath donn, of whiche we reden that at the bidding of
God, for Ismael pleyide with his brother Isaac,
550 bothe Ismael and his modir weren throwen out of the
hous of Abraham, of the whiche the cause was for by
siche pleyinge Ismael, that was the sone of the
f. 18ᵛ servant, mighte han begilid Isaac of his heretage,
that was the sone of the fre wif of Abraham.
555 Another cause was sithen Ismael was born after the

47

fleysh, and Isaac after the spirit, as seith the
apostele, to exsaumplen that pley of the fleysh is
not covenable ne helpely to the spirit but to the
bynimminge of the spiritus heretage.

560 And the thridde cause was to figuren that the
Olde Testament, that is testament of the fleysh,
may not ben holden with the Newe Testament, that
is testament of the spirit; and yif it be hooly
kept with the testament of the spirit, it doith
565 awey verre fredom and bynimmeth the heretage of
hevene. Thanne sithen the pley of Ismael was not
leveful with Isaac, myche more fleysly pley is not
leveful with the gostly werkis of Crist and of his
seintis, as ben hise miraclis to converten men to
570 the bileve, bothe for fer more distaunce of con-
trarite is bitwene fleyshly pley and the ernestful
dedis of Crist than bitwene the pley of Ismael and
Isaac, and also for the pley bitwene Ismael and
Isaac was figure of the pley bitwene the fleysh and
575 the spirit. Therfore, as two thingis most contrarious mowen not pleyn togidere withouten hurting
of either, as experiens techith, and most that party schal hurtyn that is most meintenyd, and that
partie schal be most hurt that is lest meintenyd;
580 than pleyinge that is fleschely with the werkis of
the spirit is to harming of ever either, and most
schal the fleysh hurtyn the spirit, as in suche
pleyinge the fleysh is most mei[n]tenyd and the
spirite lasse. And as in good thingis the fig-
585 uride is evermore bettere than that that is figure; so in yvel thingis that that is figurid is fer
werse than the figure; than sithen the pleyinge of
Ismael with Isaac is figure of the pleyinge of the
fleysh with the spirit, and the ton is yvel, thanne
590 fer werse is the tother. Than pleyinge with the
miraclis of God disservith more veniaunce and more
sinne is than disservyde the pleyinge of Ismael
with Isaac, and lasse yvel was; and as felaw-
[s]chip of a thral with his lord makith his lord
595 dispisid, so myche more pleyinge with the miraclis of God makith hem dispisith sithen pleyinge
to comparisoun of the mervelouse werkis of God is
fer more cherl than ony man may ben cherl of a
lord; and therfore the pleyinge of Ismael, that

600 was the sone of the servant, with Isaac, that was
the sone of the fre womman, was justly reprovyd, and
bothe the damme and the sone put out of his cumpanye;
myche more mennus pley with the mervelouse werkis of
God is reprovable and worthy to ben put out of ther
605 cumpanye.

And therfore, as seith the apostel, as ther is
no gode comuning betwene the devel and God, so ther
is no gode comuning betwene the develis instrument
to perverten men, as pleying of the fleysh, and
610 Goddis instrewment to converten men, as be his mervelous werkis, therfore, as this is a verre lesinge
to seyen that for the love of God he wil ben a good
felowe with the devil, so it is a verry lesing to
seyen that for the love of God he wil pleyen his
615 miraclis, for in neither is the love of God schewid
f. 19 but his hestis tobrokun. And sithen the serymonyes of the olde lawe, al be it that they weren
given by God, for they weren fleyshly, they shulden
not be holde with the Newe Testament, for it is
620 gostly. Myche more pleyinge, for it is fleysly,
never bedyn of God, shulde not ben don with the
mervelouse werkis of God, for they ben gostly. For
as the pleyinge of Ismael with Isaac shulde han
bynomyn Isaac his heretage, so in the keping of the
625 seremonyes of the olde lawe in the Newe Testament
shulde han bynomen men ther bileve in Crist, and han .
made men to gon bacward, that is to seye, fro the
gostly living of the Newe Testament to the fleyshly
living of the Olde Testament.

630 Myche more pleyinge of miraclis benemeth men
ther bileve in Crist and [is] verre goinge bacward
fro dedis of the spirit to onely signes don after
lustis of the fleysh that ben agenus alle the
deedis of Crist, and so miraclis pleyinge is verre
635 apostasye fro Crist. And therfore we schal nevere
findyn that miraclis pleying was usid among cristene
men but sithen religious onely in tokenes shewiden
ther religioun and not in dedis, and sithen pristis
onely in signes and for money schewiden ther prist-
640 hode and not in dedis. And therfore the apostasye
of these drawith myche of the puple after hem, as
the apostasie of Lucifer the first aungel droowgh

49

myche of hevene after him.

Yif this, frend, wil not suffisen to thee that
645 the eyghen of the blind [w]ite takun sighte, take
hede how the pleyinge of two contrary partis togidere, as of the pleyinge of the childre of Abner
and of the childre of Joab weren thre hundrid men
and sixty sleyn and mo, out of doute myche more
650 harm doth pleyinge of gostly werkis after lustus of
the fleysh as they ben more enemies. For it is of
miraclis pleyinge as it is of thes apostates that
prechen for bodily avauntage. For right as thes han
bodily avauntage at more pris than the word of God,
655 as they maken the word of God but a mene to ther
avauntage, so these miracle playeris and the fautours
of hem as they maken the miraclis of God onely a
mene to ther pley, and the pley the ende of the miraclis of God, han at more pris ther pley than the
660 miraclis of God. And so thes miraclis pleyeris and
the fawtours of hem ben verre apostaas, bothe for
they puttun God bihinde and ther owne lustis biforn,
as they han minde of God onely for sake of ther
pley and also for they deliten hem more in the pley
665 than in the miraclis silf, as an [a]postata more de-
litith him in his bodily winning than in the trowthe
of God and more preisith seemely thingis withouteforth than ony fairnesse withinneforth to Godward.
And herfore it is that siche miraclis pleyinge
670 thretith myche veniaunse of God. For right as a
jelous man seeinge his wif to japun with his kindnessis, and to lovyn by hem another man more than
him, abidith not longe to don veniaunse to chastis-
inge of hyr, so sithe God is more jelous over his
675 puple as he more lovyth it than ony man is jelous
upon his wif, he seeinge the kindnessis of his mira-
f. 19v clis put byhinde and mennus lustis beforn, and so
menis wil to ben more lovyd than his owne wille, no
wondir thof he sende sone veniaunse therafter, as he
680 moot nede, for his grete rightwessnesse and mersy.
And therfore it is that the wise man seith, "*The
ende of mirthis is sorowe, and ofte youre lawghing
shal be medelid with sorowe.*" And therfore, as experience proveth, ever sithen regnyde siche maner
685 apostasie in the puple, seside never the veniaunce
of God upon us, outher of pestilence, outher of de-

bate, outher of flodis, other of derthe, and of many othere, and comunely whan men be most unskilfuly merye sone after fallith sorowe.

690   Therfore siche miraclis pleyinge now on dayes witnessith thre thingis. First is grete sinne biforne. The second, it witnessith grete foly in the doinge. And the thridde, greet veniaunse aftir.
For right as the children of Israel, whan Moyses was
695 in the hil bisily preyinge for them, they mistristing to him, honouriden a calf of gold and afterward eetyn and drinken and risen to pleyn, and afterward weren sleyn of hem thre and twenty thousend of men. So thanne as this pleyinge wittnesside the sinne of
700 ther maumetrie beforn and her mistryst to Moyses whanne they shulde most han tristenede to him, and after ther foly in ther pleyinge, and the thridde, the veniaunce that cam after. So this miraclis pleyinge is verre wittnesse of mennus averice and
705 coveytise byfore--that is, maumetrie, as seith the apostele--for that that they shulden spendyn upon the nedis of ther negheboris, they spenden upon the pleyis; and to peyen ther rente and ther dette they wolen grucche, and to spenden two so myche upon ther
710 pley they wolen nothinge grucchen. Also to gideren men togidere to bien the derre ther vetailis, and to stiren men to glotonye and to pride and boost, they pleyn thes miraclis, and also to han wherof to spenden on thes miraclis and to holde felawschipe of
715 glotenye and lecherie in siche dayes of miraclis pleyinge, they bisien hem beforn to more gredily bygilen ther neghbors in byinge and in selling. And so this pleyinge of miraclis now on dayes is werre witnesse of hideous coveytise--that is, maumetrie.
720 And right as Moyses was that time in the hil most travelinge aboute the puple, so now is Crist in hevene with his fader most bisily pre[yi]nge for the puple; and never the latere as the ch[il]dren of Israel diden that time that in hem was, in ther pley-
725 inge of ther maumetrie, most folily to distroyen the grete travele of Moyses, so men now on dayees, after ther hidouse maumetre of coveytise in ther pleying of miraclis they don that in hem is to distroye the ententive preyere of Crist in hevene for hem, and so
730 ther miraclis pleyinge witnessith ther most folye in

ther doinge. And therfore as unkindely seiden to Aaron the children of Israel, Moyses beinge in the hil, "We witen never hou it is of Moyses, make us therfore goddis that gon biforn us," so unkindely

f. 20 seyen men nowe on dayes, "Crist doth now no miraclis for us, pleye we therfore his olde," adding many lesingis therto so colowrably that the puple gife as myche credense to hem as to the trwthe. And so they forgeten to ben percener of the prayere

740 of Crist, for the maumetrye that men don to siche miraclis pleyinge--maumetrie, I seye, for siche pleyinge men as myche honoryn (or more than) the word of God whanne it is prechid, and therfore blasfemely they seyen that siche pleyinge doith

745 more good than the word of God whanne it is prechid to the puple. A, Lord, what more blasfeme is agenus thee than to seyen to don thy bidding, as is to prechen the word of God, doth fer lasse good than to don that that is bodyn onely by man and

750 not by God, as is miraclis pleyinge? Rit forsothe as the licnesse of miraclis we clepen miraclis, right so the golden calfe the children of Israel clepiden it God, not for it was in itsilf, but for they maden it to licnesse of God, in the whiche

755 they hadden minde of the olde miraclis of God beforn and for that licnesse they worschipiden and preiseden, as they worschipiden and preisiden God in the dede of his miraclis to hem. And therfore they diden expresse maumetrye. So sithen now on dayes

760 myche of the puple worschipith and preisith onely the lickenesse of the miraclis of God as myche as the word of God in the prechours mowth by the whiche alle miraclis be don. No dowte that ne the puple doth more maumetre now in siche miraclis pleyinge

765 than dide the puple of Israel that time in heringe of the calf in as myche as the lesingis and lustus of miraclis pleyinge that men worschipen in hem is more contrarious to God and more acordinge with the devul than was that golden calf that the puple

770 worschipid. And therfore the maumetrie that time was but figure and lickenesse of mennus maumetrie nowe, and therfore, seith the apostel, alle thes thingis in figure fellen to hem, and therfore in siche miraclis pleyinge the devel is most plesid,

775 as the divel is best payid to disceive men in the

52

licnesse of that thing in whiche by God men weren
convertid biforhand and in whiche the devel was
tenyd byfornhond. Therfore oute of doute siche
miraclis pleying thretith myche more veniaunce
780   than dide the pleyinge of the children of Israel
after the heryinge of the calf, as this pleyinge
settith but japis grettere and mo benfets of God.

A, Lord, sithen childres pleyinge witnessith
ther fadris sinnes before hem and ther owne orig-
785   inal sinnes beforn and ther owne defaute of wisdam
whanne they pleyen, and ther chastising afterward
schal more greve hem, so myche more this miraclis
pleyinge witnessith mennys hidous sinnes beforn
hand and the forgeting of ther maister Crist, and
790   ther owne folye and the folye of malice passinge
the folye of childre, and that ther is grete ven-
f. 20ᵛ   iaunce to comyn to hem more than they shul mowen
paciently boren, for the grete liking that they
han in ther pley.

795   But, frend, perav[e]nture yee seyen that no
man schal make you to byleven but that it is good
to pleyen the passion of Crist and othere dedis of
him. But here agenus herith how whanne Helise
steyede up in to Bethel, childre pleyingly coming
800   agenus him seiden, "Steye up, ballard! steye up,
ballard!" And therfore he cursid hem, and two
bores of the wyilde wode al totoren of hem, two
and fourty childre. And, as alle seintis seyen,
the ballednesse of Helisee betokeneth the passion
805   of Crist, thanne sithen by this storye is opynly
schewid that men schulden not bourden with the figure of the passion of Crist ne with an holy prophete
of Crist, myche more in the Newe Testament. And
whanne men schulden be more wis, fe[r]there fro alle
810   maner pleyinge and ernestful dedis more comaundid
now than that time, and the passion of Crist more
schuld ben in drede than that time schulde han ben
Helisee. Men schulden not pleyn the passion of
Crist upon peine myche grettere than was the ven-
815   iaunce of the childre that scornyden Helisee. For
siker pleyinge of the passion of Crist is but verre
scorning of Crist, as it is seid beforn; therfore,
dere frend, beholdith how kinde tellith that the

820 more eldere a man waxith the more it is agen kinde
him for to pleyn, and therfore seith the booc, "Cursid be the childe of han hundrid yeer." And certis
the world, as seith the apostil, is now at his end-
ing, as in his laste age; therfore for the grete
neghing of the day of dome alle creaturis of God
825 nowe weryen and wrathen of mennus pleyinge, namely
of miraclis pleyinge, that most schuln be schewid
in ernest and into veniaunce at the day of dome;
therfore agen kinde of alle creaturis it is now
miraclis pleyinge, and therfore God now on dayes
830 sendith som wisdom to children than herbyforn, for
they schulden now on dayees leven pleyinge and given
hem more to ernestful werkis, plesaunt to God.
Also, frend, take hede what Crist seith in the gos-
pelle that, right as it was in the dayes of Noye
835 agenus the greet flood, men weren etinge and drink-
inge and ther likingis taking, and feerely cam the
veniaunce of God of the grete flode upon hem; so
it schalle ben of the coming of Crist to the day of
dome, that whanne men gifen hem most to ther pley-
840 inge and mirthis, ferely schal come the day of
dome upon hem with greet venianunce beforn. Therfore oute of dowte, frynd, this miracle pleyinge
that is now usid is but trewe threting of sodeyn
veniaunce upon us.

845 And therfore, dere frend, spende we nouther
oure wittis ne oure money aboute miraclis pleying,
but in doinge hem in dede, in grette drede and penaunce, for sikir the weping and the fleyshly devocion in hem ben but as strokis of han hamer on every
850 side to drive out the nail of oure drede in God and
of the day of dome, and to maken the weye of Crist
slidir and hevy to us, as rein on erthe and cley
f. 21 weies. Than, frend, yif we wilen algate pleyen,
pleyne we as Davith pleyide bifore the harrke of God,
855 and as he spac byfor Michel his wif, dispising his
pleyinge, wherfore to hir he seide in this wise,
"The Lord liveth, for I shal pleyn bifore the Lord
that hath chosen me rather than thy fadir, and al
the hous of him, and he comaundide to me that I were
860 duke upon the puple of the Lord of Israel, and I
schal pleyn, and I schal be maad fowlere more than
I am maad, and I schal ben meke in min eyen, and

54

with the handwymmen of the whiche thou speeke I
schal more glorious aperen." So this pleyinge hath
865   thre parcelis. The firste is that we beholden in
how many thingis God hath given us his grace passinge oure neytheboris, and in so myche more thanke
we him, fulfilling his wil and more tristing in him
agen alle maner reproving of owre enmys. The sec-
870   ound parcel stant in continuel beinge devowt to God
almighty and fowl and reprovable to the world, as
Crist and his apostelis schewiden hemself and as
Davith seide. The thridde parcel stant in beinge as
lowly in owre owne eyen or more than we schewen us
875   withouteforthe, settinge lest in us silf as we
knowen mo sinnes of us silf than of ony other, and
thanne beforn alle the seintis of hevene and biforn
Crist at the day of dome and in the blisse of hevene we schul ben more glorious in as myche as we
880   pleyn betere the thre forseid perselis heer, the
whiche thre perselis wel to pleyn heere and after to
comyn to hevene, graunt the holy Trinite. Amen.

56

TEXTUAL NOTES

In the text of the *Tretise* presented above, emendations are enclosed in brackets (e.g., "ch[il]dren," for MS. reading "chlyndren"). The manuscript readings and, in some instances, the readings presented by other editors are noted here.

The following abbreviations are used in the preparation of the textual notes:

MS. : British Library MS. Add. 24,202

Hudson : Anne Hudson, *English Wycliffite Writings* (1978)

Mätzner : Eduard Mätzner, *Altenglische Sprachproben*, II, 1 (1869)

---

9. Miraclis] In myraclis *MS.*; The myraclis *Mätzner*.

26. effectuel] eflectuel *MS.*

36. his] her *MS.*

51. savacioun] savacoun *MS.*

80. that] and *MS.*

82. that] ȝat *MS.*

121. but] bitt *MS.*

219. quick] quck *MS.*

254. they ben] *MS.*; be *Hudson*.

289. hatidest] hatistde *MS.*

296. al] and al *MS.*

325. matrimonye] matmonye *MS*.

348. houre] hore *Hudson*.

434. contemplacioun] contemplacoun *MS*.

472. forsothe] fosothe *MS*.

583. meintenyd] meytenyd *MS*.

594. felawschip] felawchip *MS*.

631. is verre] verre *MS*.

645. wite] pite *MS*.

665. apostata] postata *MS*.

722. preyinge] presnge *MS*.

723. children] chlyndren *MS*.

795. peraventure] peravnture *MS*.

809. ferthere] fethere *MS*.

CRITICAL NOTES

Abbreviations

Chambers   Chambers, E. K. *The Mediaeval Stage*. Oxford: Oxford Univ. Press, 1903. 2 vols.

Hazlitt   *The English Drama and Stage under the Tudor and Stuart Princes 1543-1664*, ed. W. C. Hazlitt. 1869; rpt. New York: Burt Franklin, n.d.

Hudson   *Selections from English Wycliffite Writings*, ed. Anne Hudson. Cambridge: Cambridge Univ. Press, 1978.

Mätzner   *Altenglische Sprachproben*, ed. Eduard Mätzner. Berlin, 1869. Vol. I, Pt. 2.

WB   *The Holy Bible* (Wycliffite Version), ed. Josiah Forshall and Frederic Madden. 1850. 4 vols.

The term *miraclis* as used in this treatise appears to cover a very wide range of vernacular drama of a religious nature, including plays on the Passion (probably cycle plays sponsored by civic corporations and guilds) and also plays on the lives of saints. But surely the term *miracle* as used by the author of the *Tretise* was intended to serve a polemical function; the reader is intended to see the contrast between the real miracles of Christ and his followers, and the false spectacle of the drama. The term, nevertheless, had previously been frequently used, as in Grosseteste's condemnation of plays and in Robert Mannyng of Brunne's adaptation of the *Manuel des péchés*. Thus we see that *miracles* could be used as a term of disapproval as well as approval, with the latter being suggested under the curious form *stera-*

clis in *Dives and Pauper*. (*Steraclis* combines the terms *miracles* and *spectacles*; see *OED*, s.v. *steracle*.)

3   *gospel of Jon*: John 14.6.

27-28   *bourde and pleye*: the first of these terms is synonymous with *jest*, *joke* (*OED*, s.v. *bourd*) and is also to be associated with *game*, a word often understood as indicating play even in the sense of theatrical presentation. *Playing* even among children is below in the *Tretise* (783ff) seen as inappropriate behavior indicative of the lapsarian condition. On *play*, see especially V. A. Kolve, *The Play Called Corpus Christi* (Stanford: Stanford Univ. Press, 1966), pp. 8-32, though more recent studies would qualify his analysis somewhat. Like the Wycliffite writer, even the official Protestantism of the sixteenth century in England objected strongly to playing with sacred ideas and sacred scenes in drama; see the attitude expressed in the document quoted by Father Gardiner from the Diocesan Registry at York: ". . . it is meant and purposed that in the towne of Wakefeld shalbe plaid this yere in Whitsonweke next or thereaboutes a playe commonlie called Corpus Christi playe which hath bene heretofore used there, wherein they are done t'understand that there be many thinges used which tende to the derogation of the Majestie and glorie of God, the prophanation of the sacramentes and the maunteynaunce of superstition and idolatrie; [hence] the said Commissioners [of the Diocesan Court of High Commission] decreed a lettre to be written and sent to the bailiffe, burgesses and other the inhabitantes of the said towne of Wakefeld that in the said playe no pageant be used or set furthe wherin the Ma[jes]tye of God the Father, God the Sonne, or God the Holie Ghoste or the administration of either the Sacramentes of baptisme or of the Lordes Supper be *counterfeited* or *represented*, or anythinge *played* whiche tende to the maintenaunce of superstition and idolatrie or which be contrarie to the lawes of God or of the realme" (Court Book 1575-80, fol. 19 [italics

mine], as quoted by Harold C. Gardiner, *Mysteries'
End* [New Haven: Yale Univ. Press, 1946], p. 78).
Queen Elizabeth's second proclamation against
plays insisted in 1559 that her officers should
not permit vernacular interludes to be presented
"wherin either matters of religion or of the gov-
ernance of the estate of the common weale shalbe
handled, or treated; being no meete matters to be
written or treated upon, but by menne of aucthor-
itie, learning, and wisedome, nor to be handled
before any audience but of grave and discreete
persons" (*English Dramatic Theories,* ed. Norbert
H. Platz [Tübingen: Max Niemeyer, 1973], I, 8).
Religious festivals which might be the occasions
for dramatic presentation, especially Corpus
Christi, came under attack by the more ascetically
minded, including the Lollards, long before Protestantism raised similar objections. See Hudson,
p. 25, for Lollard denunciation of Corpus Christi,
the liturgy for which is described as "untrewe and
peintid ful of false miraclis" (*Twelve Conclusions
of the Lollards,* IV).

33   *in idil:* i.e., in vain. Such use of language is
            prohibited by the Ten Commandments; see *Exodus*
            20.7.

39-46   Note the highly conservative political stance.
            The social order envisioned by Lollardy indeed de-
            pended upon aristocratic control, which it was ex-
            pected should expel the power of the pope from the
            land and establish conditions favorable to true
            religion. See the selection from the *Tractatus de
            Regibus* in Hudson, pp. 127-31. As Gordon Leff
            notes, for Wyclif "the principle of kingship was
            inherent in all forms of human association; it ap-
            plied in the church before the fall and the coming
            of endowment, when with a minimum of civil law it
            had been subject to the king's guidance. . . .
            Wyclif, although frequently reiterating the king's
            obligation to act in conformity with God's decrees,
            which was his *raison d'être,* attributed to him vir-
            tually limitless powers over his kingdom" (*Heresy
            in the Later Middle Ages* [Manchester: Manchester
            Univ. Press, 1967], II, 543-44). In this kind of

society, no *playing* of roles either above or below one's status would appear to be appropriate. For a later condemnation of role playing (1625), see Halliwell, p. 244.

67-70   *Firste . . . wittis*: the argument is from the *jest and earnest* commonplace; see the discussion in the Introduction, above, and Kolve, pp. 125ff. For Wyclif, there had been no "mixing of divine and human traditions" (Leff, II, 539); hence his followers were unable to understand how jest could legitimately be utilized for the advancement of a serious purpose. The association of playing with the flesh, desire, and the senses links together those aspects of human life which the Wycliffites, like more orthodox ascetics, distrusted most. Because playing of plays is a source of pleasurable experience for men, it is therefore of the "fleyss" as is church music (Leff, II, 576), which likewise appeals to sense and emotionally stimulates men. The distrust of man's "five wittis" stands, of course, in contrast to the emphasis on them as gateways to the soul in Franciscan and other thought of the period. See also Russell Fraser, *The War against Poetry* (Princeton: Princeton Univ. Press, 1970), p. 41, and compare Stephen Gosson's assertion in *Playes Confuted in five Actions* (London, [1582]), sig. F1^v, that playwrights "studie to make our affections overflow, whereby they draw the bridle from that parte of the mind, that should ever be curbed, from runninge on heade: which is manifest treason to our soules. . . ."

74   *of Cristis lawying*: see Introduction, above, for the Patristic source of the idea that Christ never laughed. Hudson cites Wyclif's statement "we rede not of Cristis laughtir, but of his weping we reden diverse times" (quoted by Hudson, p. 188). For the author of the *Tretise,* of course, this is a central point: jest, game, and play are symptoms of the Fall and hence are to be set apart absolutely from the sacred and from divinity. Christ, as perfect man, could hence have had no sense of humor but must have been thoroughly "ernest." Compare the anonymous *Shorte Treatise against Stage*

Playes (Hazlitt, pp. 240ff).

82-84   "*Yif . . . God*": *Hebrews* 12.8. Biblical quotations here as elsewhere do not necessarily follow
the extant Wycliffite versions of the bible exactly; such freedom in presenting the English
translation was, however, usual with Wycliffite
writers, who sometimes presented passages quite
freely translated from the Vulgate. Cf. *WB*.

104-06   "Be yee . . . him": *I Peter* 5.6-7.

111-13   "hidous . . . live": not St. Peter's words, but a
passage from *Hebrews* 10.31, which reads in *WB*:
"It is feerful for to falle into hondis of God
livinge."

129-30   *And sithen . . . gospel*: *Matthew* 6.24; *Luke* 16.13.
As Gosson later indicated, there should be no
idea of a truce between God and the devil (sig.
B4).

138-40   "Eche . . . mourninge": *Hebrews* 12.11.

140-41   *veine sightis of degyse, aray*: here the controversial subject of costume, which is essential to
dramatic presentation, is introduced. Distrust of
disguise within a play was something that later
made even Shakespeare uneasy, for in his *Macbeth*,
for example, he established his guilty hero's vil-
lainy through the imagery of stolen and ill-fit-
ting clothing; the Scottish tyrant in the end of
the play becomes a mere actor exhibiting outward
show and inward emptiness. Through costume, actors appear to be something they are not. The
spectacles in which such costumed actors take part
are, according to the Wycliffite writer, "veine
sightis" since they allegedly lack the substance
of reality. The later sixteenth and seventeenth-
century enemies of the stage would have agreed, as
would many earlier writers, including of course
Herrad of Landsberg. Hence in Prynne's opinion,
any attempt to appear something other than what
one is--e.g., "the common *accursed hellish art of
face-painting*"--involves sinful falsification; God

"enjoi[n]s all men at all times, *to be such in shew, as they are in truth: to seeme that outwardly which they are inwardly;* to act themselves, not others. . ." (*Histriomastix* [London, 1633], p. 159). See also Jonas Barish, "The Antitheatrical Prejudice," *Critical Quarterly*, 8 (1966), 332-33. With regard to medieval practice, considerable evidence concerning costumes and masks is to be found in the dramatic records such as those transcribed for York by Johnston and Rogerson for Records of Early English Drama (Toronto: Univ. of Toronto Press, 1979), 2 vols.

142   *stiring . . . to leccherie:* playing, since it is the source of pleasure through experiences entering through the senses, is associated with the body and with the flesh; the latter, along with the world and the devil, should be forsaken in the rite of baptism. Also associated with the flesh is, of course, *gluttony,* which is mentioned later in the sentence along with "othere vicis" which likewise function to draw the mind away from the urgency of the spiritual realities. The sins of the flesh would appear to have provided the principal temptation of the theater for such early critics as Tertullian. See also Introduction, above.

144   *debatis:* see Herrad of Landsberg's insistence that at plays the conclusion of the entertainment is often rowdiness: "Rarely does such a gathering break up without quarrelling" (quoted in Chambers, II, 98n). Some less than pious behavior would also seem to have been recorded in Friar William Melton's remarks in 1426 (*York,* ed. Johnston and Rogerson, I, 43; II, 728), for he complains about "feastings, drunkenness, clamours" as well as singing and other insolent actions on the part of the revelling persons in the city at the time when the plays are presented. Melton, however, defends the value of the plays, which he in no way finds offensive. It would be hard to believe that the revellers were more than an obnoxious minority, especially since we can discover from the records that there was great concern that the plays should

64

be presented without embarrassing incidents that detract from the honor of the city.

147   *yerde of God over his heved*: reminiscent of statements made elsewhere by ascetic writers, who maintained that bodily delights should be entirely given up by those who give themselves over totally to spiritual thoughts and actions. See, for example, the story of the man who fell into the abyss in the *Golden Legend* in the section devoted to the saints Barlaam and Josaphat: though the bush (i.e., human life) to which he clings is being gnawed away at its roots by mice (temporality), he becomes enraptured by some honey dripping from the bush and forgets about all danger. The honey is, of course, the pleasurable experience available in this world which leads men to forget the ever-present reality of man's precarious state. The rod or "yerde" of God is, of course, the rod of judgment which will condemn the unrighteous.

155   *Pharao*: see *Exodus* 7-12.

157-58   *the Jewis that bobbiden Crist*: hot cockles, or "*the bobbid* game," is described by the writer in MS. Bodl. 649 (as quoted by G. R. Owst, *Literature and Pulpit in Medieval England* [Oxford: Blackwell, 1961], p. 510) as "a common game in use nowadays . . . which the soldiers played with Christ at his Passion. . . ." The writer continues:

> In this game, one of the company will be *blindfold* and set in a prone position; then those standing by will hit him on the head and say--
>> "*A bobbid, a bobbid, a biliried: Smite not her, bot thu smite a gode!*"
>
> And as often as the former may fail to guess correctly *and rede amis*[s], he has to play a fresh game. And so, until he *rede him that smote him*, he will be *blindfold stille and hold in* for the post of player.

The game is identified as "papse" in the York cycle and "whele and pylle" in the N-town plays;

both cycles, along with the Towneley plays, utilize this game for the presentation of the Passion. See the discussion of this game in relation to the vernacular plays in Kolve, pp. 185-86. For a list of available illustrations of hot cockles, see Lilian W. C. Randall, *Images in the Margins of Gothic Manuscripts* (Berkeley and Los Angeles: Univ. of California Press, 1966), p. 111. On the anti-Semitism implicit in this passage and in the plays generally, see Stephen Spector, "Anti-Semitism and the English Mystery Plays," *Comparative Drama*, 13 (1979), 3-16.

168   *to halowyn his name*: the command implicit in the invocation at the beginning of the Lord's Prayer.

174-76   The nature of the devotional response to the plays is here established as consistent with the affective spirituality prevalent, particularly in the countries in the North of Europe, in the late Middle Ages. See Clifford Davidson, "Northern Spirituality and the Late Medieval Drama of York," in *The Spirituality of Western Christendom*, ed. E. Rozanne Elder (Kalamazoo: Cistercian Publications, 1976), pp. 125-51, and also the Introduction, above. The display of emotion, particularly upon viewing an image, was hardly new, however; note, for example, the instance of Gregory of Nyssa who was brought to tears each time he saw a certain image showing the Sacrifice of Isaac, which of course typologically represents the Crucifixion of Christ on the cross (Gerhart B. Ladner, "The Concept of the Image in the Greek Fathers and the Byzantine Iconoclastic Controversy," *Dumbarton Oaks Papers*, 7 [1953], 4). Art and drama, however, shared a common aim in the late Middle Ages in their attempt to present the Passion of Christ *feelingly*, even to the point of "bitere teris." Michelangelo is reported to have sneered at such expression of Northern piety in response to Flemish painting; such works, he is believed to have said, might well bring tears to the pious' eyes, though on the whole those who thus responded were "women, young girls, clerics, nuns, and gentlefolk without much understanding for the true harmony of art" (quoted in Erwin Panofsky, *Early Nether-landish Painting* [Cambridge: Harvard Univ. Press, 1953], I, 2). This kind of piety also offended Protestants--a response which is reflected in the description of Corpus Christi day with its procession and plays in Barnabe Googe's *The Popish Kingdom* (London, 1570), fols. 53v-54. Here it is complained that "Christes passion here derided is, with sundrie maskes and playes," including pageants "playde in worship of this bred [of the Eucharist],/ That please the people well." The streets are strewn with rushes and decked out for the occasion, and strangers fall upon their knees in devotion. Father Gardiner additionally cites another important reference, though it is from the post-Reformation period in a Catholic territory, in which Mme. d'Aulnoy in a letter in 1679 indicates "that she saw the audience fall on their knees and strike their breasts when the character of St. Anthony said his *confiteor* on the stage" (*Mysteries' End*, pp. 18-19).

211-19   This statement has been interpreted to indicate that the writer actually approved of certain images--a stance more moderate than the usual Wycliffite position which tended to encourage iconoclasm (cf. Hudson, pp. 83-88). In any case, these sentences are perhaps among the most important in the *Tretise*, for they establish a direct linkage between drama and the scenes of the visual arts; see also Clifford Davidson, *Drama and Art* (Kalamazoo: Medieval Institute, 1977), pp. 12-13. That this connection was a commonplace one, with theatrical presentation seen as having certain advantages, is also indicated in Reginald Pecock's *The Repressor of Over Much Blaming of the Clergy*, ed. Churchill Babington, Rolls ser., 19 (London, 1860), pp. 216-22. Pecock (p. 221) suggests that a Crucifix of wood or stone in "the likenes of Crist hanging on a cros nakid and woundid" is the best means of coming to understand Christ in his "manhode"; the only more effective means is "whanne a quik man is sett in a pley to be hangid nakid on a cros and to be in seming woundid and scourgid." Unfortunately, he

laments, plays showing the Passion are staged
"ful seelde and in fewe placis and cuntrees."

234   *folc of avoutrie*: see *Matthew* 12.39.

241   *Anticrist*: on the obsession with Antichrist
among Wyclif and his followers, see Leff, II, 520,
541. Like many Protestants in the sixteenth century, they tended to see the official Church as
an arm of the powers of darkness. See Clifford
Davidson, "Wyclif and the Middle English Sermon,"
*Universitas: A Journal of Religion and the Univer-
sity*, 3 (1965-66), 92.

245   *signis withoute dede*: see Introduction, above,
for comment on the relation of this charge to the
current philosophical trends, especially nominalism. The sign detached from reality in mimesis,
of course, was a point upon which the Church Fathers had attacked dramatic representation, and
in the Renaissance the deceptiveness of such
representation was again under attack. See Fraser, *War against Poetry*, pp. 3-51. The charge
of "idilnesse" is one that also appears in the
sixteenth century (e.g., in Stephen Gosson's
School of Abuse, a book which labels players "the
Sonnes of idlenesse" [quoted by Fraser, p. 59]).

249-52 *to pristis . . . pleyinge*: Hudson, p. 188, notes
that the Wycliffite *Floretum*, an alphabetical
listing which includes an entry under *histrio,*
cites canon law on this matter; additionally, she
makes reference to decretals which forbid the
participation of clergy in theatrics. Some of
the medieval legislation against the drama is
noted by Gardiner, pp. 4-19. Fraser (p. 42) re-
peats A. P. Rossiter's quotation from the Dean of
the Faculty of Theology at Paris in the fifteenth
century who condemned "priests and clerks" who
run and leap through "the whole church in unblush-
ing shameless iniquity" or drive "about the town
and its theatres in carts and deplorable carriages
to make an infamous spectacle" (*English Drama from
Early Times* [1950; rpt. New York: Barnes and Noble, 1967], p. 59). But it is hard to know here

precisely what theatrical activity is being condemned, though surely included are the Feast of Fools, games in the churchyard, and other activities commonly criticized. Pageant processions seem to be indicated, but we cannot be sure what kind are meant. See also Rosemary Woolf, *The English Mystery Plays* (Berkeley and Los Angeles: Univ. of California Press, 1972), pp. 81, 363. Earlier Church councils had, of course, condemned clerical participation, as in the case of the synod at Tours in 813 which declared that the clergy ought to flee "the obscenity of the players and the scurrilities of debased jesting" (quoted by Allardyce Nicoll, *Masks, Mimes, and Miracles* [London: George G. Harrap, 1931], p. 147). But such prohibitions were later seldom interpreted to include quasi-dramatic rituals and liturgical drama, and it is also questionable how far the usual clergyman would normally have seen them directed against vernacular drama primarily devotional in character. Woolf, p. 363, quotes a gloss to the decretals of Gregory IX which excludes from condemnation plays on subjects which "conduce to devotion rather than to lasciviousness and delight of the senses." At York, the author of the Creed Play was almost certainly a chantry priest named William Revetour, whose role we may assume was not untypical in the presentation of civic drama. Revetour's will, quoted in *York*, ed. Johnston and Rogerson, I, 68 (trans., ibid., II, 746), also refers to stage props associated with the play which are contributed along with the book containing "le Crede Play" to the Guild of Corpus Christi. See also Alexandra F. Johnston, "The Plays of the Religious Guilds of York: The Creed Play and the Pater Noster Play," *Speculum*, 50 (1975), 57-59.

254   *ypocrisie*: cf. Prynne's demand that we see *hypocrisy* as a word which signifies "*but the acting of anothers part or person on the Stage:* or what else is *an hypocrite, in his true etimologie, but a Stage-player, or one who acts anothers part. . . . And hence is it, that . . . sundry Fathers . . . stile Stage-players hypocrites; Hypo-*

crites, Stage-players, as being one and the same in substance. . ." (*Histriomastix*, pp. 158-59). The evidence from "*sundry Fathers*" of the Church is supplied in Prynne's footnote, p. 158.

262-64   "*Not . . . kindam*": *Matthew* 7.21.

277-80   Hudson notes: "The distinction is between the sin itself which is evil, as was the sin of Adam or the rejection of Christ by the Jews, and the response of God to this evil action through which good results. The paradox is expressed neatly in the lyric *Adam lay ybounden . . .*" (p. 188).

288-89   "Turne . . . vanitees": Psalm 118 (119).37.

289-90   "Lord . . . vanitees": Psalm 30 (31).7, which the Wycliffite version gives (quoted by Mätzner, p. 231): "Thou hatedist aboute waiteris vanites over-veinliche." On the liturgical use of this passage and of lines 288-89, above, see Hudson, pp. 188-89.

296-97   *as a jay . . . himsilf*: cf. Thomas Wright, *The Political Songs of England* (London, 1839), p. 328:
> For riht me thinketh hit fareth by a prest
>   that is lewed,
> As by a jay in a kage, that himself hath
>   bishrewed. . . .

302-03   *many men . . . peine*: the reference here has not been convincingly traced, but see Hudson, p. 189. Perhaps the writer is merely jeering at those who do not take seriously enough the threat of hell fire.

312-14   "Lord . . . person": *Tobit* 3.14-17, following the Vulgate, "Nunquam cum ludentibus miscui me," which in the Wycliffite version appears as "Nevere with pleyeres I mengde me" (quoted by Mätzner, p. 231).

322-41   The Wycliffite writer's extended attention to priests taking part in plays, or otherwise encouraging them, provides additional evidence that the clergy did indeed play a role in the religious theater of the time. That the role was a key one is further suggested by various sources, including the direct connection, noted above in a previous note, between the Creed Play at York and the chantry priest William Revetour of St. William's Chapel in that city.

326-28   *alle othere sacramentis . . . Crist*: the writer's view of the sacraments, especially of the Eucharist, seems here quite orthodox. Cf. Hudson, pp. 107-15.

330   *quen of Saba . . . Crist*: see *Matthew* 12.42.

349-50   *pley of Anticrist . . . Dome*: Antichrist appears only in the Chester cycle among the extant medieval English plays, but there is an important continental play on the subject from an earlier date reprinted in Karl Young, *The Drama of the Medieval Church* (Oxford: Clarendon Press, 1933), II, 371-87. See additionally the discussion in John Wright, ed., *The Play of Antichrist* (Toronto: Pontifical Institute of Mediaeval Studies, 1967), which also provides a translation of the continental play. The Chester Clothworkers' and Dyers' plays of *Antichrist's Prophets* and *Antichrist* have been edited most recently by R. M. Lumiansky and David Mills in *The Chester Mystery Cycle*, EETS, s.s. 3 (1974), I, 396-438. The Judgment play, which more often than not apparently concluded each cycle, appears at the end of the four extant cycles in Middle English. At York, the Doomsday play was given by the Mercers, the most affluent of the local guilds, who were able to provide a spectacular close to the cycle. See Alexandra F. Johnston and Margaret Dorrell [Rogerson], "The York Mercers and Their Pageant of Doomsday, 1433-1526," *Leeds Studies in English*, n.s. 6 (1972), 10-35. Choice of these plays for the Wycliffite writer's jibe is probably determined more by his obsession with Antichrist and the end of time than by his direct observation of actual plays.

352-54   "*Do . . . rightwise*": *Romans* 3.8, for which *WB*
          reads: "Do we yvele thingis, that goode thingis
          come. Whos dampnacioun is just."

363-64   *Crist . . . passioun*: *Luke* 23.28. The author's
          argument against *holy tears* is critical; see note
          to 174-76, above.

401-02   "Thou . . . swetnesse": Psalm 20 (21).4.

409-10   *ypocritis and lieris*: a traditional charge which
          later would, of course, be again repeated by cri-
          tics of the stage in Sidney's time. On hypocrisy
          and actors, see note to 254, above. Sidney's re-
          futation of the accusation that the poet/play-
          wright is a liar may be found in his *Defense of
          Poesie*, which insists: "Now, for the poet, he
          nothing affirms and therefore never lieth" (*Liter-
          ary Criticism: Plato to Dryden*, ed. Allan H. Gil-
          bert [1940; rpt. Detroit: Wayne State Univ. Press,
          1962], p. 439). Gosson had insisted that plays
          "are no Images of trueth," since "they handle
          such thinges as never were" or they distort real-
          ity (*Playes Confuted*, sig. D5).

427-28   *for othere mengid trewthis . . . yvel*: this pas-
          sage is glossed by Hudson as follows: "for others
          mixed truths (with lies), and make that which is
          really evil to be considered to be good."

430-35   *what recreacioun . . . vanite*: the Puritan ob-
          jection to Sunday games and recreation of other
          kinds is well known; the Wycliffite writer's at-
          titude surely foreshadows this aspect of Puritan-
          ism. See the chapter entitled "Sabbatarianism"
          in M. M. Knappen, *Tudor Puritanism* (Chicago: Univ.
          of Chicago Press, 1939), pp. 442-50. But ascetic
          hostility to recreation through the Middle Ages
          has been well established.

436-37   *werkis of mercy*: the corporal acts of mercy de-
          scribed in *Matthew* 25 and commonly depicted in
          art, as in the famous window in All Saints, North
          Street, York (see Clifford Davidson and David E.
          O'Connor, *York Art* [Kalamazoo: Medieval Institute

Publications, 1978], pp. 116-17). The corporal acts were at the heart of catholic attitudes toward charity in the late Middle Ages--attitudes that suffered under the Protestant condemnation of "works righteousness" in the sixteenth century. For the Wycliffite writer, such sincere *acts* are to replace the hypocritical and lying *actions* of the drama and theater.

448   *bokis to lewid men*: a direct reference to the opinion, definitively set forth for the West by Pope Gregory to Bishop Serenus of Marseilles, that "a picture especially serves as a book [pro lectione] to the common people" (quoted by Woolf, pp. 87, 365).

456   *An half frynde*: the second part of the *Tretise* begins here. Very likely, because of the shift in tone and the identification of a different audience, it is to be regarded as a separate item entirely. It is specifically directed to the "half frynde" who, while he sympathizes with Wycliffite attitudes and doctrine, refuses to reject plays though these are here allegedly condemned by Lollards generally. This portion of the *Tretise*, designed to convince the "frynde" of the wrongness of his opinions and actions with regard to playing and patronage of plays, is more distinctively heterodox than the first part of the work. See the dissertation by N. Davis, pp. 103-04.

457-58   *Thomas of Inde*: the apostle, who according to medieval accounts such as the *Golden Legend* became a missionary to India. His scepticism is, of course, proverbial, for he would not believe in the risen Christ until confronted with him; thus the "half frynde" will not stay away from plays or otherwise refrain from supporting them until confronted with proof from holy writ and the doctrine derived from it.

490   *hadden or lassen*: see *Deuteronomy* 12.32. Mätzner (p. 235) quotes the Wycliffite version: "ne adde thow eny thing, no lasse."

513   *heritage*: salvation, presented here allegorically in terms of a deed or document giving one the right of ownership to property. Cf. George Herbert's seventeenth-century poem, "Redemption," which likewise treats salvation in terms of rents and leases.

527-28   "Wo . . . good": *Isaiah* 5.20.

537-39   *Adam . . . therof*: it was worse to attempt to conceal the transgression than to commit it in the first place.

549   *Ismael pleyide*: see *Genesis* 21.9ff, esp. verse 9 in the Vulgate rendering: "Cumque vidisset Sara filium Agar Egyptiae ludentem cum Isaac filio suo. . . ."

556   *fleysh . . . spirit*: see *Galatians* 4.29-30.

606-09   *ther is . . . men*: see *II Corinthians* 6.14-16: "Sothly what partinge, *or comuninge*, of right-wisnesse with wickidnesse? or what felowschip of light to derknessis? sothly what acordinge of Crist to Belial?" (*WB*).

640-43   *the apostasye . . . him*: i.e., as Lucifer drew many angels to follow him at the time of his fall, so apostate priests command the loyalty of a high percentage of the people (who indeed would insist that they are being properly devoted to the interests of the Church and the divine commands). As hypocrites, such priests, like Lucifer, have something in common with stage players, who also outwardly pretend to be something that they are not. Note the Chester Playwright's Dominaciones, who tell Lucifer upon his rebellion that he has "begone a parlous playe" (Play 1, 1. 207).

647-49   *the pleyinge . . . mo*: see *II Samuel* 2.14-31.

681-83   "The ende . . . sorowe": *Proverbs* 14.13, which Mätzner quotes in one Wycliffite version: "Lawghing schal be medlid with sorewe . . ." (p. 238).

74

694-98   *the children . . . men*: *Exodus* 32.6; cf. *I Corinthians* 10.7: "The peple sat for to ete and drinke, and they han risun up for to pleye" (*WB*).

705-06   *as seith the apostele*: see *Colossians* 3.5.

707-08   *spenden upon the pleyis*: extant dramatic records are indicative of the very substantial expenditures made in support of civic drama such as that sponsored at York, Coventry, and other cities. For some suggestions with regard to the economic conditions which made such expenditures possible and apparently desirable, see Carolyn L. Wightman, "The Genesis and Function of the English Mystery Plays," *Studies in Medieval Culture*, 11 (1977), 133-36. There is no reason whatever to believe that the expense of the plays was regarded as a burden, except when a guild declined in wealth and/or numbers.

716-17   *they bisien . . . selling*: the sponsors of the plays were hardly always able to separate spiritual profit from economic profit gained from the festivities which brought a large crowd of outsiders to the city on such occasions as Corpus Christi day. As the plays themselves demonstrate, there was clearly great difficulty experienced in distinguishing the sacred from the profane, for so thoroughly was the world sacralized through rite and image. The Wycliffite writer, however, sets out to make very clear distinctions indeed between the secular and the profane on the one hand, and the sacred on the other; the first of these categories he associates with the flesh, the second with the spirit. In spite of natural weaknesses, men are to set their minds upon the sacred to the exclusion of all else; the plays are, as they would have been for Plato in ancient Greece, distractions which take the mind away from reality.

733-34   *"We witen . . . us"*: *Exodus* 32.1.

741-46   *siche pleyinge . . . puple*: perhaps an attack on the Franciscan view which, while valuing preaching highly, nevertheless saw playing as a more vivid kind of sermon; see David L. Jeffrey, "Franciscan Spirituality and the Rise of the Early English Drama," *Mosaic*, 8, No. 4 (1975), 25-34. See also Owst, pp. 471-547, and Woolf, p. 367, for additional discussion of the relation between drama and sermon material, and additionally Davidson, "Wyclif and the Middle English Sermon," pp. 92-99, for Wycliffite attitudes toward homiletic practice. As late as Philip Stubbes' *Anatomy of Abuses* the opinion that the plays may "be as good as Sermons" is put forth only to be confuted as "blasphemie intollerable" (Halliwell, p. 222). For Stubbes as for the writer of the Wycliffite *Tretise*, religious plays are to be regarded as much less tolerable than secular productions (see ibid., p. 118).

752-54   *the golden . . . licnesse of God*: see the defense of images in the 82nd canon of the Council of 692 which authorized realistic or at least anthropomorphic representations of the deity as opposed to the merely symbolic since it was held that the former had more educational and ritual value than the latter (Kitzinger, "The Cult of Images in the Age before Iconoclasm," *Dumbarton Oaks Papers*, 8 [1954], 142). The golden calf, however, can hardly be seen as an anthropomorphic image or in any non-symbolic sense made in "licnesse of God"; the writer of the *Tretise* is intent upon attacking the idea of the devotional image, and in so doing takes up an Old Testament example of idolatry that is not as exact as logic would perhaps demand.

762-63   *the word of God . . . don*: the Word is for the Wycliffite to be identified with the Word of *John* 1. This identification would later also be made widely by the Protestants, especially the Puritan ministers of the late sixteenth and the seventeenth centuries who likewise saw the final result as the conversion of the soul through encounter with the Word in the course of hearing it preached (see, for example, John Cotton, *Gods Mercie Mixed with his Justice* [1641; rpt. Gainesville, Florida, 1958], p. 120). The devotional image, especially in drama where language is joined to spectacle, is therefore rejected as a source of conversion or of strengthening of the faith.

772   Cf. *I Corinthians* 10.11.

783-84   *childres . . . hem*: see Kolve, pp. 28-29, and Philippe Ariés, *Centuries of Childhood*, trans. Robert Baldick (New York: Knopf, 1962), pp. 71-72. The latter indicates, especially in his chapter on games and pastimes, how children tended to play adult games after the age of about five or six. There was, as Ariés points out, tremendous pressure on the child to join the adult world. The Wycliffite writer, however, would deny to the child as to the adult the activity of playing games, since it involves something other than sincere movement or action on the part of the players. *Jest* is clearly to be replaced by *earnest* at the earliest possible age.

798-803   *how whanne . . . childre*: *II Kings* 2.23-24; the authorized version's wording "and mocked him" involves a departure from the Vulgate "et illudebant ei," which of course directly provided the source for the Wycliffite writer.

804-05   *the ballednesse . . . Crist*: possibly from a play on words based on the Vulgate's word for *baldness*, for the text in the Latin gives the children's jeers as "Ascende calve, ascende calve" (*II Kings* 2.23).

820-21   "*Cursid . . . yeer*": *Isaiah* 65.20.

824   *day of dome*: there is here an expectation of the Last Day, which is felt to be imminent. Orthodoxy, though it sometimes drew some different implications from the "grete neghing of the day of dome," nevertheless considered it a tenet of belief which provided the basis for the final play of each of the extant Middle English cycles.

834-39   *as it was . . . dome*: see *Matthew* 24.38-39. Typologically, the Flood was normally regarded as foreshadowing the Last Day, when those who were more concerned with eating and drinking-- i.e., with the things of the flesh--would again be destroyed. But for orthodox thinking, the ark is normally a symbol of the Church which would provide sufficient safety for those who are on board. The Wycliffite writer extends the usual warning--a warning implicit in the Doomsday plays of the great mystery cycles--to those also who separate the sign from the reality in play as in the stage presentation of religious drama.

849-50   *strokis . . . side*: cf. the visual depictions of warnings against swearing and sabbath breaking in which the crucified Christ is shown surrounded by various tools and instruments, as in the fif- teenth-century wall painting at Breage, Cornwall.

857-64   *"The Lord . . . aperen"*: *II Samuel* 6.21-22: "And David seide to Michol, 'The Lord liveth, for I shal pleye before the Lord, that hath chosen me rather than thy fader, and than al the hows of him, and he hath comaundid to me, that I were a ledere upon the puple of the Lord of Israel; and I shal pleye, and fowlere I shal be maad more than I am maad, and I shal be meke in min eyen, and with hoond wymmen, of the whiche thou hast spoken, more glorious I shal apere'" (*WB*).

GLOSSARY

Since the words glossed are those which might cause difficulty to potential users, the object has been to provide information with the least amount of complexity. Hence complete lexicological information has not been included, and the spelling reflects actual usage in the *Tretise* and in the quoted passages from Middle English in the Introduction. In the glossary, *y* has been treated as *i* alphabetically when it is indicative of a vowel and not a consonant.

abiten, *abide, persevere*
agen, agens, agenys, agenus, *(prep.) against, toward, in opposition to*
agenward, *on the contrary*
algate, *(adv.) always and at all events*
anentis, *(prep.) concerning*
aperen, *appear*
apostata, *(n.) apostate, person abandoning his religious belief;* apostaas, *(n., pl.) apostates*
aray, *(1.) an arrangement in order, (2.) clothing or costume*
assayen, *attempt*
assoile, *grant absolution*
aughten, *ought*
avauntage, *advantage*
avoutreris, *adulterers (esp. in religious sense, i.e., heretics*
avoutrie, *adultery, heresy*
axen, *ask*

bad, *see* bedyn
ballard, *bald person*
ballednesse, *baldness*
bedyn, bodyn, *bidden, commanded;* bad, *(3sg. pret. ind.)*
begilid, bygilen, *beguiled, deceived*
benemeth, bynimith, bynomen, *take(s) away from;* bynimminge, *(pr.p.)*
benfets, *(n., pl.) benefits, things well done*
bern, *burn*
bethinking us, *considering*

79

bien, *buy, purchase;* bying, *(pr.p.)*
bileve, byleve, *belief*
bynimminge, *see* benemeth
bynomen, *see* benemeth
bysien, *busy, make (themselves) active*
bisily, *(adv.) solicitously*
bisinesse,*(n.) solicitude*
bourde, *(n.) jest, joke, game*
bourdfully, *(adv.) jestingly, playfully*
bourdith, bourden, *jest, joke, play;* bourdinge *(pr.p.)*
brynning, *(adj.) burning*
blonder, *confusion*
bobbiden, *struck (with fists)*
bodyn, *see* bedyn
booc, *book, i.e., the Bible*
boost, *(n.) boasting*
boren, *(p.p.) bear*
bores, *(n., pl.) boars*

certis, *(adv.) certainly*
cherl, *churl*
clepith, *calls*
comenden, *recommend*
comynte, *community*
comuning, *communing, having in common*
continaunse, *self-restraint, esp. with regard to sexual con-
    trol*
contunuely, *(adv.) continually*
covenable, *suitable, appropriate*
cristen, *(adj.) Christian*
cure, *spiritual charge or office*
curious, *elaborate, expensively wrought*

damme, *mother (contemptuous)*
dampnable, *condemned*
dampneth, *condemns*
dampning, *(n.) damnation*
debatis, *strife, quarrels*
dede, deede, *deed, actuality;* dedis, *(n., pl.) deeds*
deed, *(adj.) dead*
defaute, *defect*
degyse, *disguise, i.e., costume wearing*
demyen, demyn, *judge*
derre, *dearer*
deth, dethe, *death*

dette, *debt*
develiche, *devilish*
dilitid, *delighted*
dispitouse, *cruel*
distruyith, *destroys*
doyinge, *(n.) action*
don, donn, doun, *do, done;* doying, *(pr.p.) doing, making;*
    dude, *did*
dom, dome, *doom, judgment*
doutouse, dowtous, *uncertain, doubtful*
drede, *(n.) dread*
dredyn, *(v.) fear*
droowgh, *(v.) drew*

eyen, eyghen, *eyes*
eld, *(adj.) old*
enmys, *enemies*
ensaumplide, exsaumplide, exsaumplid, exsaumpplid, *(v.) dis-
    played, set forth as examples (to be followed)*
ententive, *heedful*
enterly, *fully*
entirlodies, *interludes, plays*
equite, *fairness, equity*
Estryn, *Easter*
everelastande, *everlasting*

fadir, *father;* fadris, *(n., pl. gen.) fathers'*
fautours, fawtours, *patrons*
feerely, ferely, *(adv.) altogether, commonly (in a group)*
fer, *far, much*
figure, *(n.) type, pre-figuring*
figuride, *type, that which foreshadowed*
figurid, figuren, *(v.) pre-figure, foreshadow*
fleen, *(v.) flee, escape*
fleyinge, *fleeing, escaping*
fleysh, fleyssh, fleyshe, fleysche, fleyss, *flesh, the body
    as opposed to the spirit*
fleyshly, fleysly, fleschely, *(adj.) fleshly*
foly, folye, *folly*
forbedun, *forbidden*
furthe, *fourth*

gabben, *(v.) jeer*
gamen, *games*
gideren, *gather*

gin, *trap;* ginnys, *(n., pl.)*
gladen, *become glad*
gostly, *(adj.) spiritual*
grete, grette, gret, *(adj.) great;* grettere, *greater*
grevys, *groves*
grucchen, grucche, *complain*

hadden, *(v.) add, increase*
han, *have*
han, *(art.) an*
harrke, *ark (of the covenant)*
hauteyn, *(adj.) haughty*
heie, *(adj.) high, great*
Helyse, Helisee, *Elisha*
helpely, *helpful, affording help*
hem, *(pron.) them*
henhaunce, *enhance, raise up*
hennys, *hence*
herynge, herying, *praising, worshipping*
herith, heren, heeren, *hear;* heringe, *(pr.p.) hearing*
Heroudis, *Herod*
hert, *heart*
hest, heste, heest, *command;* hestis, *(n., pl.) commands*
hethene, *heathen, non-Christian*
heved, hevyd, *head*
hide, *heed*
hidous, *terrible, dreadful*
hyinge, *hastening*
hog-hyerd, *swineherd*
holde, holdun, *compared*
homely, *(adv.) familiarly*
hond, *hand;* hondis, *(n., pl.) hands*
hool, *(adj.) whole*
hooly, *(adv.) entirely*
hopiden, *(v.) hope*
hore, houre, *(pron.) their*

ypocrisie, *hypocrisy*
yvel, yvele, *evil*

jape, japun, *(v.) jest, trick (sometimes with the sense of seduce)*
japeris, *(n., pl.) tricksters*
japing, japinge, *ribaldry*
japis, *(n., pl.) tricks, ribaldry*

japinge stikke, *a laughing stock*

kindam, *kingdom, i.e., heaven*
knowechist, *(v.) have knowledge*
kunning, *(n.) knowledge, learning*

lasse, *(adj.) less*
lassen, *(v.) decrease*
latere, *latter*
lawying, lawghing, *(n.) laughing*
leesith, *loses*
leeve, *cease, fail;* leevinge, *(pr.p.) failing*
lefully, *(adv.) allowably*
lesing, leesing, *lie, untruth;* lesingis, leesingis, *(n.,
      pl.)*
leute, leaute, *(n.) faith*
leveful, leeveful, leful, *(adj.) allowable, lawful*
leven, leevyn, *reject;* leving, *(pr.p.) rejecting, turning
      aside from*
liyn, *lie*
likingis, *(n., pl.) pleasure*
lovelich, *beautiful, implying kind*
lowen, lowyn, *(v.) laugh*
lust, *desire;* lustis, lustus, *(n., pl.) desires*

maad, *made*
maintenours, *supporters, patrons*
mannisch, *(adj.) human*
maumetrie, maumetre, *idolatry*
mawmete, *idol*
mede, *(n.) reward, with possibly a suggestion of bribery*
medeful, *merit*
medelid, medelyd, *(v.) mingled, mixed*
meintenid, meintenyd, *sustained, supported*
mekid, *made meek, humbled*
menes, *means*
mengid, mingid, *mixed, confused;* menging, *mixing (in a con-
      fused way)*
mennus, mennis, *(n., pl. gen.) men's*
mete, *food*
myche, *much*
mistryst, *distrust*
mistristing, *distrusting*
mo, *more*
modir, *mother*

morning, *mourning*
mot, moot, moten, *must*
mowen, *may, might*

ne, *nor*
nedis, *needs*
neghen, neghing, *approaching, nearing*
neibore, neiebore, *neighbor;* neieburs, neytheboris, *(n., pl.)*
noon, *(adj.) no*

obeschaunce, *obeisance, obedience, submission*
ocuped, *(v.) engaged*
on live, *alive*
onys, *once*
oon, *one*
outher . . . outher, *either . . . or*

parcel, *part;* percelis, perselis, *(n., pl.)*
party, partie, *part*
peintid, *painted*
peinture, *painting*
peraventure, *(adv.) perhaps (by chance)*
percener, *partaker;* perceneris, *(n., pl.)*
pere, *equal (in the social order)*
perilis, *(n., pl.) dangers*
pris, *(n.) price, value in money*
pristis, *(n., pl.) priests*
Psauter book, *psalter, book of psalms*
puple, *people*

quick, *living*

reden, riden, *(v.) read, implying also to attend to*
regnyde, *ruled*
rein, *rain*
reprovable, reprowable, *reprehensible*
riden, *see* reden
rit, *right*
ritwesnes, rightwessnesse, *righteousness, rectitude*
rightwise, *righteous*

savacioun, *salvation*
schewid, *shown, revealed*
schrewidnesse, schrewidenesse, *wickedness, maliciousness*
sechith, sechen, *seek(s)*

84

seeld, *seldom, rarely*
seyn, *seen*
seint, *saint;* seintis, *(n., pl.)*
seith, *says*
semen, *seem, appear*
sentense, *authoritative opinion*
serymonyes, *ceremonies*
seside, *ceased*
settith, *sets, establishes*
shrewe, *villain*
shrewyn, *(v.) scold or curse*
shrewinge, *scolding or cursing*
siker, sikir, *(adv.) surely*
singnys, *(n., pl.) signs*
sith, sithen, sithis, *since*
sleeth, *(v.) kills*
slidir, *(adj.) slippery*
sodeyn, *sudden*
sofisen, suffisen, *suffice*
sone, *son*
sorwing, *sorrowing*
sothely, *(adv.) truly*
spedely, *quickly*
spiritus, *(n. gen.) spirit's*
stant, *consists*
steryn, *stimulate*
steyede, *(v.) went (up);* steyen, *rise;* steyinge, *(pr.p.)*
    rising, i.e., climbing; steye, *(imper.) go up*
suerte, *certainty*
suffraunce, *long-suffering, endurance*
swyche, siche, sich, *such*

tac, *take*
tariere, *(n.) lingerer*
tenyd, *(v.) grieved*
thenken, *(v.) think, consider*
teris, *tears*
thanne, *then*
ther, *(pron.) their*
tho, *(pron.) those*
thof, *though*
threting, *threatening*
thretith, *threatens*
thridde, *third*
thurgh, *(prep.) through*

tide, *time*
to, *too*
tobrokun, *(adj.) broken, disobeyed*
togydere, *together, at the same time*
tokenes, *(n., pl.) (outward) signs*
ton, *one*
tooc, *took*
totoren, *torn apart*
traveile, travele, *labor (sometimes oppressive)*
traveilinge, *laboring*
travelous, *oppressive, wearisome*
treytyn, *take, handle*
tristenede, *trusted*
tristing, *trusting*
trowe, *believe*
trowthe, trwthe, *truth*
trwe, trewe, *(adj.) true*

unknowing, *not knowing*
unleful, *prohibited*

veniaunce, veniaunse, *vengeance*
verry, verre, verrey, werre, werry, *(adj.) actual, true*
verre, verely, werrily, *(adv.) actually*
vetailis, *(n., pl.) victuals*
vilenye, veleynye, *indignity, dishonor, malice*
vois, *voice*

wantown, *wanton, unrestrained*
waitinge, *(adj.) attendant*
watte, *(imper.) know*
waxen, *grow*
wede, *(v.) become insane*
weilen, *lament*
wenen, *(v) think*
wery, *weary*
weryen, *tire;* weryinge, *(pr.p.) wearying*
werinesse, *weariness*
werre, werry, *see* verre *(adj.)*
werrily, *see* verre *(adv.)*
whanne, *when*
wherthoru, *whereupon*
wyilde, *wild*
wymmen, *(n., pl.) women*
wite, *(n.) sense, mind*

witen, *(v.) know;* woost, *(2sg. pres. ind.)*
wode, *wood*
wolden, *would*
wonninges, *(n., pl.) dwellings*
woost, *see* witen
worchen, worschen, *(v.) work*
wrathen, *(v.) become unwilling, resist*
wrooth, *unwilling*

yerd, yerde, yird, *rod*
yif, *(prep.) if*
yilding, *giving up*
yole, *Christmas*